PRAISE FOR *I*

It is always refreshing and rewarding to read inspirational books, particularly those that are authentic accounts reflecting the lives of faithful and exemplary Christians such as Joel Esperance who have excelled. He has done an outstanding job sharing with honesty his upbringing, struggles, desire to succeed, and big accomplishments. This is an uplifting book that sheds great insight and will help the reader to see the extraordinary things a person can achieve when determined to trust God and seek His guidance.

Dr. Frank Moreno Director Language
Division Florida Baptist Convention

Congratulations on the publication of your first book, *I Sat Where You Sit*. I believe it to be the first of many books you will be blessed to author. It is insightful, compassionate, funny, and it speaks a message ... There is nothing that is too difficult for our GOD!

Dr. Marvin Wells, D.M.D.
Surgeon
Well Oral & Maxillofacial
and Surgery Association

Every once in a while God gives to His people a man who is serious about the challenges of day to day living with its ups and downs. Today we are especially challenged because the pattern for life is so distorted, we have forgotten, they that will live Godly will yet suffer. Your book (I Sat Where You Sit) has shown perseverance and will pay off.
God Bless you, Joel, my friend.

Bishop Chorrethers Jenkins,
Overseer of SOY Faith International

Joel Esperance has written an account of his life which is both gripping and heart warming. He writes with clarity and unusual honesty about how God has been with him throughout a life of high mountain peaks and low valleys. He has lived a full life and doesn't hesitate to share the joy and pain of a life lived in God's service.

In addition, Joel's book provides important insights in how to cope with both success and failure. His story is not so much about an exceptional man, but rather of a common man who through hard work, determination, and perseverance accomplished exceptional things. *I Sat Where You Sit* will inspire you to appreciate God's presence in the seemingly small and everyday affairs of life.

Dr. Michael Riley

When Joel Esperance makes this statement *'I Sat Where You Sit'*, he takes you on a journey and an adventure that the reader can identify with. He is sharing real life; the problems, struggles that we will go through and how God is in control the whole time. At time you will laugh, you will cry and rejoice that God has a wonderful plan for your life and He is in control. Enjoy the journey!

Dr. Herman Rios, Director
Language Evangelism & Stewardship Department
Florida Baptist Convention

I SAT WHERE YOU SIT

I SAT WHERE YOU SIT

JOEL ESPERANCE

Tate Publishing & Enterprises

Published by Tate Publishing & Enterprises, LLC
127 E. Trade Center Terrace | Mustang, Oklahoma 73064 USA
1.888.361.9473 | www.tatepublishing.com

Tate Publishing is committed to excellence in the publishing industry. The company reflects the philosophy established by the founders, based on Psalm 68:11,
"The Lord gave the word and great was the company of those who published it."

Book design copyright © 2011 by Tate Publishing, LLC. All rights reserved.
Cover design by Kristen Verser
Interior design by Stefanie Rane

Published in the United States of America

ISBN: 978-1-61663-945-7
1. Biography & Autobiography, Personal Memoirs
2. Biography & Autobiography, Religious
11.02.22

ACKNOWLEDGMENT

First and foremost, I am thankful to God Almighty for His abundant grace and mercy. It is a blessing, and I thank Him for granting me the privilege and the intelligence to write this book. I am hopeful that the book will help readers understand that they are not being singled out. Whatever problems or situations that they are facing, I hope they will bare in mind that: "someone sat where they sit" & "that too shall pass." I am convinced that every day that I wake up is a blessing.

I have so much to be thankful for and so many to whom I need to give thanks for being there for me. So I can be sure that I don't leave anyone behind, I thank my family, my parents, my siblings, my friends, and all acquaintances that have impacted my life directly and indirectly. Formally, I would like to thank my mother, Manmie Jo, and all of my siblings, biological and adopted, for their constant love and continuous support. I want to thank my wife Kéké and the boys, Joey and Ricky, for their profuse *love* and *affection*. I want to thank Kettline's parents, those who are alive and those who did not live to hear about and/or read this book.

I would not be able to write this book without the direct and indirect support of the following people that impacted my life. I will try to collectively and individually acknowledge everyone; however, if anyone knows that they have done something for me or have helped me in anyway, and feel that they should have also been acknowledged, I am sorry. But, I can tell you that your support, help, and encouragement were well received and are not, and will not be, forgotten.

Thanks to Brother Avelant Pierre for lending his only pair of shoes to me to go to Port-au-Prince for my secondary school entry exam. Thank you to Brother Rene Sylvestre for braving and protecting us during one of the worst hurricanes (Flora) to ever strike Haiti. Thanks also for helping the family in many ways while my dad, Papa Joe, was hospitalized long-term. To Marie France Dalencour, thank you for helping me get my first job, your tireless managerial and morale support, and in particular for making ample sacrifices to visit me in the hospital, General Hospital of Port-au-Prince, and in my house several times after my release from the hospital. Mrs. Dalencour, I will be forever thankful and grateful to you. To Dr. Christian Duclerville, one of the best surgeons in the world, I thank you for saving my life. To Bruno Botti, thank you for giving me a job that lasted for twenty-six years and also for giving my wife her first job ever. Mr. Botti has not only helped me, but also my brother Jarman and his wife, and my sister Marie France to secure employment in the early eighties in Ohio. To Rosanne Klonaris, thank you for being a great and long time friend. Thank you for always making time to listen or talk to me when I needed advice and/or counsel. Mrs. Klonaris is an example of a genuine friend, someone sincere and honest. I value our friendship. To Reverend Gerard Pierre Mirbel, thanks for being a long time friend and for your sincere devotion to my family. Thank you to Pastor Pierre and his family, in particular his late mother, Sister Sylvanie Augustine, who babysat my boys for many years, a million. He also took the boys to school from Pre-school to ninth grade, babysat them, and cared for them while Kettline and I were going to school for higher education. To Castane Simeon-Dacilien, my mother in-law, thank you for taking care of our boys from birth to toddler and helping us in the house as well. To the Haitian Community in Ohio/Illinois, thank you for being a second family for me and for each other. You have helped me to live with confidence and joy day after day. Even when I am not around them, I never feel alone, because they make it so that I can always feel their presence. I am honored to be a member of this group, the best group of friends in the world. To the late Max Pierre Gaujean and his wife, Emmelyne, thank you for your genuine and honest love and support. I will not ever be able to detail everything you've done for me and my family. Dr. Gaujean was my best friend. Not only I am privileged to call him my friend, I am honored. Max encouraged me to write this book and I know he would have been the first to read it. Life is not fair, but God is good. His favorite motto was: *"You are not the first, you won't be the last."* Max was my hero.

To Mr. Al. G., thank you for helping me to further my career and your guidance. If it were not for you, I would not have an MBA today. Al helped me even when I rebelled against his advice. I learned so much from him, but I realized what he did and meant to me too late. Not only do I thank him, but I also apologize and ask for his forgiveness. I hope that he forgives me. Al was a true friend and hopefully, one day, we can be friends again. I will always be grateful to him. He was my mentor and coach for more than twelve years.

Last but not least, I want to thank one more person that I will leave unnamed. I thank her for her exceptional friendship and her genuine appreciation. She was there for me during the worst time in my life, which included my atrocities and adversities in the year of 2008. If it were not for her, I would not have made it through. She came to my life to assist and to provide me with guidance and support. She helped me psychologically, emotionally, and spiritually. She stood by me and I can openly say that she was one of the people that trusted me with everything they had.

While I am thanking people that come and/ or came to my life for a purpose, I would like to thank, in particular, a friend that came into my life just to send a poem to me: "People come into your life for a reason, a season, or for a life time" that would help me understand why, today, I thanked the last two friends in past tense.

Finally, to the Floridians of Jacksonville, I thank you for making my move to Jacksonville joyful and prosperous. In particular, I want to thank Mrs. Pamela Quales for opening the door of the city so I could meet the great Dr. Edith Abdullah and Dr. Kathryn Birmingham, who in turn gave me the opportunity to apply for a position at the college and subsequently work there.

I thank them from the bottom of my heart. "Last but not the least," to Dr. Marvin Wells, my brother *in-love,* "Mon Frère" as he calls me, thanks a million for providing a bundle of support during my transition from sabbatical back into the workforce in Florida. Dr. Wells and his family made sure that my spiritual and financial needs were met. At the end of my contract with the college, Dr. Wells hired me full time so I could provide for my family financially. He did not have to do that. Marvin is a great Man of God. He would have done this for anyone, but of course, for his brother he went farther. *In Jesus' name, Amen!* as Marvin would say.

I would not like to close without thanking the friends that helped build and support my two organizations, Omega–5 and HCBF (Haitian Coalition for a Better Future) and that became good friends of mine: Bishop C.M. Jenkins, Rev. Gerard Pierre Mirbel, Rev. Joseph Desir, Pastor Olian Saint Jacques, Ms. Nancy Brown, Ms. Aline Pierre Louis, Mr. Anthony Petruzzi, Ms. Krista Zivkovich, Mr. Francky Sterlin, Mr. William Arsene, Ms. Berta Emile, and Ms. Guerlande Valme.

In conclusion, I would like to thank Tate Publishing Company for publishing my book. To my friend, Dr. Feyla Lamothe, thank you for reading and editing my final draft. Feyla, I appreciated all suggestions and recommendations you have given to me. Without them, this book would not have been as effective as I had intended it to be. Thanks to Paul Holly, dba (DJA) my friend from Africa, for reviewing the French/Creole portions. To all family, friends, and acquaintances who have encouraged and supported me to write this book and to those I didn't individually and/or personally mention by name, thank you, thank you so very much.

God bless you all.

TABLE OF CONTENTS

"God has a purpose and a plan for everyone's life. So, no matter how tough things get, don't quit"

BIRTH TO 9-YEAR-OLD

Born in Petionville, Haiti West Indies

I was born in Petionville, Haiti, West Indies, on April 18, 1953. Allow me to tell you a little bit about my native country. On December 5, 1492, Christopher Columbus, discovered the Hispaniola Island in the West Indies. Haiti covers the western third of the island and lies between Cuba and Puerto Rico in the Caribbean Sea. The Dominican Republic covers the eastern two-thirds of the island. Most of Haiti is mountainous, and the country's name comes from an Indian word that means "High Ground." The climate is warm. Haiti, with a population of 9,035,536 (2009 estimate), is the most populous and least developed country in the western hemisphere. It covers an area of 10,714 square miles (27,750 square kilometers).

Haiti is the oldest black republic in the world and is also the second oldest independent nation in the Americas. Haiti obtained its independence on January 1, 1804, while the U.S. declared theirs on July 4, 1776. Unfortunately, most of the time Haiti has been ruled by people disinterested in the welfare of the Haitian people. The official name of the country in French is *La République d'Haïti*. Its capital and largest city is Port-au-Prince with a population of 1,961,107 (2009 estimate). The Haitians' native language is Créole, and their official language is French. Most Haitians, or eighty percent, belong to the Roman Catholic Church, seventeen percent belong to the Protestant Church, and two percent practice voodoo. However, many in the church believe in the practice of the African religion, voodoo.

Concerning the city where I was born–Pétionville–it has a population of 106,369 (2005 estimate), and it is located five miles west of Port-au-Prince; it is considered one of the most glamorous cities of the country, where many of the elite class live. In addition to Pétionville, Miragoâne, which is located in the southern part of the country, is another area that is important in my story. Miragoâne is about 55 miles south from Port-au-Prince. It has a population of 90,000 (2005 estimate). I spent a great deal of my childhood there.

My Parents

I was born into a large, Christian family. My parents got married March 15, 1947. At that time, my dad was a plumber and my mom was a housewife. Dad would go to work, most of the time in the provinces (outside of the city). My mom would stay home to care for us. Their dream was to serve the Lord and to have their own place of worship. They began to pray about it, and the Lord led them to form their own church. Today, Dad is a retired pastor, three brothers and two sisters are pastors, and one of the brothers is currently pursuing an advanced pastoral degree at the University of Indiana. My dad had two sons, Jean-Claude and Serge Robert, before he was married. The Lord has blessed Mom and him with seven more children, three sons and four daughters.

The seven children are as follows: Giscelaine, Ruth, Paul, Joel-Fils, (me), Jarman, Marie France, and Marie Nicole.

My brother Jean-Claude died in 1985. He was a great guy. I loved him very much. My brother Robert is one of the pastors.

As I am writing this book, Dad is ninety-five years old and Mom is eighty-two years old. They are now living in Saint Petersburg, Florida. I always wanted to know how my parents started their ministry. So, I asked them to explain how they became involved in the ministry. They told me that when my brother Paul was four months old, they would have prayer in their bedroom each night before they went to bed. One night, while sitting in the living room waiting for Dad to come back from work, my mom heard a voice say, "Tonight, you are not going to pray in the bedroom, but right here where you are."

When Dad came back, she told him about the voice. Dad was perplexed. He only said, "It is okay with me." That night they prayed in the living room.

The next morning, a woman in the neighborhood told Mom that she heard them praying and that she wanted to join them, but was afraid to knock on the door and also realized she was not dressed appropriately. Mom invited her to join them the next night for prayer. The following night the neighbor brought her entire family. God blessed the gathering, and every night they had more attendees. Dad asked his local pastor to let him use his church for evening prayer services. The pastor said yes. Dad and Mom gradually started a small church by using the pastor's fellowship hall. At that time, Dad was still a deacon of his local church. Because of the size of his group, Dad started a church on his own. Then he decided to enroll in pastoral training in a Bible school. After two years of holding worship services, Dad looked for spiritual and technical support from a senior pastor. By then I was born, and my dad thought that I was the one to replace him one day, so he named me after himself, "P'tit Joel." Lucky me!

The pastor that Dad contacted for help did not do him a favor. Instead, the senior pastor divided the church and kept the majority of the members. Dad was so upset that he threatened to quit the ministry all together. My mom, who was not ready to give up all, asked the remaining members to rejoin them and to start over. Only one-fourth of the members left with Dad. Not only that, but the members that left with my dad also took all the church furniture and brought them along to the other place of gathering.

My mom moved to another location with the members, where they had services under a tent in someone's backyard. Dad was too upset. He did not want to be part of the small gathering. Six months later, they found a place to rent, and an American pastor, Pastor Hummer, paid for the hall. Mom and the members were very happy. They decided to ask Dad to come to see how they were doing and asked him to join them. The hall cost $20.00 a month plus $2.00 for electricity. Things were not going well for my family financially, and they could not even afford that small amount. By then I was a year old. Pastor Hummer helped Dad get back on his feet. Then the group started to grow rapidly. Unfortunately, the joy was not going to last. A year later things turned sour. There was a conflict between my parents and Pastor Hummer, which led to a division. Once again, the church was split. That was another devastating blow for Dad.

As the saying goes, "Behind every great man, there is a great woman." Once again, Mom made a comeback. She contacted another American pastor, Pastor Charles, in late 1954. My brother Jarman was just born. Pastor Charles was very receptive of the invitation, but he was hesitant to invest too much time and money in the ministry. However, the ministry started to grow. People were being saved, and within two years they had to find a larger place to worship. My folks were having a blast; they thought this was really it. Suddenly, things turned sour again. The devil stepped in and entered Pastor Charles's heart. He did exactly what Pastor Hummer had done. He split the church. There is no need to tell you how my folks felt.

Before the latest division took place, Dad had become a full-time pastor and was in process for his ordination. This time, things were different. Dad did not let circumstances drive him away from the ministry. Through some friends in Haiti, he contacted the Assembly of God mission representatives in the U.S. and asked them to come and help him rebuild the church in Haiti. The mission responded quickly, and within a few months they came to Haiti to help Dad rebuild the church. The Assembly of God paid for everything in full including the building, the necessary furniture, and the accessories for the ministry. That was how the Assemblies of God Mission started in Haiti. I can proudly say that because of the efforts of my folks, the mission was introduced in Haiti in 1956. Coincidently, my brother Jarman was the Superintendent and General Director of the Assembly of God Mission in Haiti from 1994 to 2004. Don't tell me that God is not good. Later in the book you will see how God works mysteriously in my family's life, and more particularly, in my life.

Unfortunately, as always, it was not as easy as Dad thought it would be. Things were still too complicated. For some political reasons, Dad lost control of the church and he found himself facing the same decision that had hurt him so much in the past. He realized that it was not only his family that would be hurt if the church was to split, but all the members would be hurt. Dad decided to do it differently. He left the mission without splitting the church. He could have, but he chose not to.

One of the proverbs from the French author, Alfred de Musset, said, *"Nul ne se connaît tant qu'il n'a pas souffert."* If I were to translate this proverb in English, I would say: "You don't know what you are made out of, until you face some adversities." You will realize why my folks went through all that pain. God had a plan for them, and He was testing them to assure Himself that they would be ready for what lay a head.

In about 1958, Dad joined a small mission by the name of Emmanuel Holiness; a move that was good for the entire family and that would last for four years. During that period, we had plenty of clothing, shoes, and food. By the time we joined the Emmanuel Holiness, I was about five or six, and I could clearly remember that my parents would receive a number of containers full of clothing every two to three months. At the same time, they also would receive cases of food that included rice, beans, milk, cheese, corn beef, sausages, Karo syrup, and other items. Oh! Life was beautiful. My parents would give clothes, shoes, and food to non-Christians and Catholics on Mondays and to the Protestants on Saturdays. I had so many shoes, mostly cowboy boots; and I had so many blue jeans. No one would ever believe it. I think that the clothes and shoes came from Texas, because of the cowboy boots and the style of the shirts. When we had to go somewhere, everyone in the family would wear cowboy boots. I don't quite remember it, but my parents told me that I would always hide clothes and shoes to pass to my friends and their families, even though my friends' families would receive their portions during regular food and clothing distributions; but that did not matter to me, I would still give them some more later. We were at a high point of our lives with plenty of clothes to wear and plenty to eat. Meanwhile, Dad was going back and forth to Miragoâne on mission trips planting churches. Once again, I am asking you to bare in mind the province of Miragoâne, because you are going to hear plenty about it.

In 1960, I was seven years old. I learned my first hard lesson for doing something stupid. Actually, I thought I had learned a lesson then, but you will find out that I have not learned a thing. Here we go! It was a beautiful afternoon. The temperature was perfect. There was a nice breeze, the sun was about to go down, and the atmosphere was calm and radiant. My parents were entertaining a few visitors on the front porch. I was playing in the backyard with a few friends. I decided that I wanted to buy a *Boul Sinlo* (lollypop). So I went to the front porch and signaled my mom to catch her attention. She made a motion and asked me to come to talk to her. I asked her for ten cents. She told me that she did not have the money. Then right after talking with me, she called Iranie, a nanny who was working for us at that time, to come get some money so she could buy a pack of coffee powder to make coffee for the guests. My mom put the money on a small table that was within a few feet of where they were talking, so that Iranie could get it when she was ready to go out to buy the coffee.

I took ten cents out of the money and began to play with it on the ground. A few minutes later, I buried the money purposely so that my mom would think that she did not give enough money to Iranie. Iranie notified my mom that she would not be able to buy the coffee because ten cents were missing. Without missing a beat, my mom called, "P'tit Joel."

"Oui maman," I answered.

"Bring the money back right now."

I did not say anything. I ran outside to look for the money. Unfortunately, I forgot where I buried it. I knew right away that I was in trouble–big, big trouble.

Then she called me a second time, with a loud voice, "P'tit Joel come here."

"Here I am, Mom."

"Did you take ten cents out of the money that I put on the table?" she asked.

"Me, take the money? I saw the money, but I did not take the money," I responded.

My mom began to get upset. She said, "You better tell me if you took it, because if I find out that you took it, *I will kill you.*" Obviously, she did not mean literally *kill* me. She meant that she would sanctify my *derriere* with a belt.

At that time I told her that I was playing with the money and accidentally buried it in the backyard. Mom asked me to search the whole area, which I did. Unfortunately, after a good fifteen minutes, I could not find it, so Iranie came in my rescue.

She was watching me and saw where I put the money. She began to look in the target area. It did not take her even a minute to find the money. I thought that I was saved but my mom told me that she was going to whip me in a way that she had never done it before. Then she said, *"Qui vole un oeuf, volera un boeuf"* (Once a thief, always a thief). Mom administered a whipping with a belt to a point where one of our neighbors, Mrs. Adele Beauniface, came to rescue me from my mom's grip. You would think by now I would have learned my lesson. No. No. I did not, because in the next few years, I would make another attempt to steal, except this time it would not be money but a piece of meat.

The organization, Emmanuel Holiness, offered a great opportunity to my dad, which he turned down for a seemingly ridiculous reason. That mistake would morally, mentally, and almost physically destroy the entire family. The offered deal was that Dad would take over the organization and receive a monthly salary plus allowances for utilities, maintenance expenses, and a trip to the U.S. once a year to discuss the organization's progress. Since the organization was small and young, they would not pay the assistant pastor, who happened to be a close friend of the family. Dad decided it was not right that the organization would not pay a salary to his assistant. He declined the offer. No one could understand why Dad made a "stupid" decision like this and what exactly his logic was behind it.

The closest reason that I could come up with for his decision, unless it was an act of God, was the fact that Dad, years ago while working as a plumber, had a close working relationship with a Mulatto family that I will call LaCross. The LaCrosses immigrated to Haiti from France, and later on they were naturalized as Haitians. They were very active in engineering and politics. They were among the famous five percent elites in the country and, of course, they were living in Petionville. There is no need to say that the elites of Haiti are predominantly white or very light-skinned. When Dr. François Duvalier (Papa Doc) became president of Haïti in 1957, he quickly demolished the elites' power.

The majority of the LaCross family fled Haïti voluntarily, and some were arrested and jailed in the following years. So because of my dad's affiliation with the LaCross family, he probably was looking for a way out of the area. Either that or God himself, to prevent and protect our lives, prompted Dad to decline the offer.

At that time, Dad did not have very much of a choice. He had to leave the organization. He later joined the Pentecostal Church of God Mission, which was and still is probably the poorest denomination abroad and in the U.S. Our life was a perfect example of a roller coaster. This decision would put us back in miserable circumstances. Dad would remain a pastor for them for over thirty-five years, and he would eventually get fired because he spent too much time in the U.S., while placing an assistant pastor in charge to run the churches in his absence. The mission headquarters' management removed Dad from the church for desertion and replaced him without notice. Dad lost the house and the land where we lived, and the church was divided once again, for the last time.

For some reason or another, Dad was not happy with the church, the country, life, and probably himself. This situation continued for a couple of years. The mission's administrators would dictate and reprimand him, a situation he had never been in before. Dad was still planting churches in Miragoâne, and he was spending more time there.

As I mentioned previously, when Dad found out that some of the LaCross families were in trouble, depression and fear of Papa Doc's rampage forced him to move indefinitely to Miragoâne, where our lives would change for the worst of the worst. The family was not happy with the move, but Dad left anyway for Miragoâne in December 1960. We stayed in Port-au-Prince for school, but we would spend the entire 1961 summer vacation in Miragoâne. Things began to get very complicated; Dad was not home, Mom had to make monthly trips, and there were two houses to care for. So, a big decision was going to take place: The boys (including me) would end up staying in Miragoâne after spending the 1962 summer vacation. Dad could have picked a better place to put us, but instead we found ourselves four kilometers south of the downtown Miragoâne in a two-room house with no electricity and no running water. The kitchen, bathroom, and commode were all outside. Don't get me wrong. The place was fine for vacation, but living there year-round was a different ballgame.

Although, during vacation some of us slept in the church, the following summer of 1963 was different and seemingly permanent. The entire family stayed in Miragoâne for good. Some adjustments would be made. Two rooms were added to the house, but still my brother Jarman, Jean (foster brother), Antonio (gardener), and I would sleep in the church. Let me add that there was nothing covering the doors or windows in the church, and that would be where I would be sleeping until I was sixteen. My other brothers Jean-Claude, Robert, and Paul would go back to Port-au-Prince during the school year for secondary school. My life took a complete turnaround and at that time, I was nine-years old.

NINE YEARS OLD TO SEVENTEEN YEARS OLD

Life in Miragoâne

The southern city of Miragoâne is located about fifty-five miles from Port-au-Prince. It has a population of approximately 90,000. I have asked you to keep Miragoâne in mind. I hope you did. The reality began to kick in, moving from the number one city of the country to the mountainside, from the light to the dark, from a fairly large house to a two-room, thirteen by thirteen square foot hut with three doors (one in the front, one in the middle wall, and one in the back). If you stood in front of the house you could see the backyard, if the doors were wide opened. There was one side door and two windows. We had neither plumbing nor electricity. There were no schools or places to work. Everyone worked his or her land for food. Basically, everyone was a farmer. They sold some of their crops to area merchants or buyers so they could use the money to buy other food to cook and other necessities.

Right behind the house there was a small shaded ten by ten square foot area that served as a kitchen. No need to tell you that we did not have a stove. We had to use a handmade grill, kind of a small barbecue grill. The grill was only used when Mom cooked. On the other hand, when the servants cooked, they would use three big rocks that would sit in a triangle shape that served as support to the cooking pot. Dried wood and small tree branches would be set between the rocks in a way that they would join together. They would be lit and fanned until they produced a healthy fire. Thirty feet from the other side of the house, there was a smaller hut that served as a latrine or commode.

Let me clear something for you about the servants' situation. I am pretty certain that you wonder how we could afford to employ maids. In order to illustrate this scenario for you, I will have to tell you a story: Once upon a time, a poor, poor man. After so many months of eating almost nothing, he realized that he had three, small sweet potatoes left to eat. Not only that, he knew that was the last that he was going to have. He made a tough decision that he was going to eat them all and hang himself. He baked them under hot sand, because he did not have a pot to boil them. He climbed on a tree, made the noose, and sat on a branch of the tree. He pulled the potatoes and peeled them, dropped the skins down, and he ate the potatoes. He then placed the noose around his neck and made his last wish. Before jumping, he took a look down, probably to see how far he was from the ground, when he realized that while he was peeling the potatoes the skins had dropped on someone else who ate them all. With the noose on his neck, he made a reflection: "He must be worst off than I am, because I had potatoes while he did not get anything. So, why am I killing myself?" He changed his mind and did not try to hang himself. This is to say there were people that were far poorer than we were. That was why we could afford to hire maids.

In Miragoâne, there were a lot of mango trees, sugarcanes, and plantain bananas growing everywhere. There was one main road that ran from west to south, and it was unpaved. Although a short portion of the road from the capital city to Carrefour, going toward Miragoâne, which is approximately eight miles, was barely paved, the other forty-seven miles were dirt roads. One can imagine that it would take only an hour to drive from Port-au-Prince to Miragoâne. Oh no! At that time it would take six to seven hours to make it by bus and four or five hours traveling in private four-wheel drive vehicles, providing the roads are dry and good. During the rainy seasons, most people would not make it home on the same day of travel. Please note that the roads that I am talking about were the main roads that connected one major city to another and one small city to another. There were many pathways, which were created by people and their horses, mules, and donkeys. The majority of people used horses as a way to travel and mules and donkeys to transport their crops and belongings from point A to point B. Those pathways were as wide as two or three feet. Most of the time those pathways would have corn or whatever crops were growing at that particular season on both sides of them. Most people who traveled those pathways would walk barefoot.

That adjustment was difficult in many ways for us. A few years before, we were at the prime of our lives. We had a lot to wear and plenty to eat. Now, I would wake up in the morning and I was responsible to find something to eat. Each day, I went to the farm and would look for avocados, fresh corn on the cob, sweet potatoes, mango, and watermelon to bring home. I baked corn and sweet potatoes, set them in a plate, sometimes a few plates if I had enough to share. Our normal breakfast was consist of "grinding corn" (like grits) with avocado and sometimes also with anchovy. You can say it again: "Disgusting!" "Yikes!" For lunch, it was more corn or mangos. Most of the time, we had one special meal per day. Monday through Saturday, we would have one these cereals: *maïs, petit mil, gros mil, ou riz.* We cooked them with dry or green beans. Sometimes we had dinner with pureed beans, rarely with meat. On Sunday, we had white rice, plantains, and dry, pureed. Sometimes we had red, black, or white pureed beans, but most of the time we had green pureed beans. As for meat, we had chicken, goat, or beef.

My first Christmas in Miragoâne, December 1962, was quite an experience. Beginning on Christmas Eve, Dad let us know that we would have to go to church for a midnight service. Then, we would have gifts on Christmas morning. I called a few friends in the neighborhood and invited them to the service, but I let them know that was the only night that we could spend out. My friends and I put a plan together. We would go to church and have a party after the service. What we did that night would remain a tradition for many years to come. We bought a pint of "*Clairin*" (alcohol, 95 percent proof). We mixed it with lemon and sugar to make a powerful liquor for the *fiesta*. We would save it in a small stream of water that Dad used to water the farm. Our intention was to keep it cool. From what I can remember, Christmas Eve was always the brightest night; you could find a needle if it fell on the ground. There were a few oil lamps in the church. People walked four or five miles to come to church that night. I had to sit in the church from 7:30 p.m. to 12:30 a.m. Wow, that was long! But we had a great service. People sang regular songs and Christmas carols. We prayed and gave thanks to God throughout the service.

After the service, Dad gave us the okay to spend the rest of the night out. I went straight to get the drink and brought it right back into the church. We did not know where else to go. We sat in the church talking, drinking, and singing till we all passed out. I woke up to find Dad holding his long belt and wanting an explanation. Since I could not come up with one, Dad administered "*une fessée*" (a whipping) to me. The tradition that stayed was not drinking in the church, but the drink itself. I was supposed to get a capsule pistol and a little plastic car for

Christmas. Unfortunately, as a way of further punishment, I did not get them.

December 31, 1962, was another experience, the same situation as Christmas Eve, but after the midnight service we were supervised, but that did not stop us from getting our drinks. What was different on New Year's Day? Children got dressed in a new garment and would go from house to house wishing people Happy New Year, and adults in the house served them cake and liquor. Sometimes the liquor would contain a high level of alcohol, but the adults served it to kids anyway. After the treat, they also gave them some money. I used to compete with my brothers and my sisters to see who got more money on those particular days. That same year, I got lost. I went too far and I got to drink too much liquor. I got drunk and forgot my way home. At that time, my dad sent a few people to look for me. They found me very drunk with a pocket full of money and far away from home. At home, Dad was waiting for me at the door with his favorite long belt. Guess what? I got another "fessée" (a whipping).

The year I turned ten years old, 1963, was a year that the whole family will never forget. Early in the school year, I woke up very early every day to get ready to school. As I mentioned before, my house was about four or five kilometers from the school. School started at eight o'clock in the morning. It would take approximately one hour to walk that distance. During winter, it was very cold. The grass was covered with frost, and the water was cold. You can guess how life would be miserable when you had to take a shower or a bath in cold water. The only beauty at that time was we had maids. At times, our maid Madame Luc was paid less than fifteen dollars a month, including room and board. Anyway, the maid offered to warm the water before I took a bath in the morning. But Dad always encouraged us to take a cold shower instead so that we could be strong and less likely to get sick. Madame Luc would prepare a weird breakfast, which at time was wonderful and tasty. Breakfast was a kind of ground dry corn, like a very coarse grits, cooked also like grits, which would be served with anchovy sauce and avocado. Believe it or not, I still eat this kind of breakfast once in a while. Then, she would also prepare a lunch that we could take with us.

At that time, school lasted all day. Classes were from eight o'clock until noon, then there was a one-hour recess, and then classes would resume from one o'clock until four o'clock. We would eat lunch during recess, and we also would do a lot of stupid things to kill the time. But as it happened, one of those stupid things saved my life. Because the school was so close to the sea, when the tide came in, it would run in the schoolyard. At lunchtime, a few of us would go in the water to bathe and learn how to swim. There was a very small island, approximately a hundred and fifty feet from the school building. Between the school and the island, the water was about fifty-five to sixty-five feet deep. We would try to swim to the island and back to the school on a daily basis.

One day I had to run some errands. I had to go around the main customs area, pretty close to the main dock. When there were not any boats docked there, people would go and walk around to look at the sea. The water was clear and was about thirty-five feet deep, but because of the clarity of the water, one could see the sand at the bottom.

Downtown Miragoâne is down a hill a half-mile deep from the top. To enter the city, the road forks into two roads, which are called *Carrefour La Croix*. The two roads are *Bel Air* and *Nouvelle Cité*. While standing on the dock, you could see *Bel Air* up the hill. On that particular day, while I was walking on the dock, I spotted a friend of mine who was walking toward downtown from *Bel Air*. My friend and I were trying to talk to each other by signs and gestures. Meanwhile, I was walking backward and for a minute I forgot where I was. Suddenly, it felt like I was flying and the next thing I knew, I heard a big splash. There I was in the water. I plunged to about twenty-five feet. I believe that I lost consciousness for a very short time. I managed to get out of the water. Thank God that I spent some time learning how to swim. I almost lost my life.

We used to form groups to go to and from school. There were five major schools in Miragoâne. Two of them were free Catholics Schools, *Une Ecole des Soeurs* and *Une Ecole des Frères*, two were private schools, and one was *Une Ecole Publique*, free or minimum pay. I was in one of the private schools and later on was transferred to the National School, where I graduated from elementary grade level, or seventh grade.

In that same year, another funny thing happened to me. My brother Jarman was attending a very small local Christian school in the area where we lived. So, he did not have to go downtown every morning. There was a group of eight to twelve girls who attended the Catholic Girls' school. Those girls would do anything and everything to make my life miserable. They used to call me *Cuff Moulin*. I never knew and to this date I still don't know what the heck *Cuff Moulin* means. If you remember in the last few pages, I described the position of their school compared to mine. They would be up the hill and I down the hill. Or they would be at *Bel Air* and I would be at *Nouvelle Cité*. These two streets meet at *Carrefour La Croix*, and that road would take us to Chalon, where most of us lived. I used to be so afraid of them that if I realized that I was walking ahead of the girls, I would run like a chicken so they would not catch up with me. And if the girls realized that I was ahead of them, they would run until they could catch up with me. The trouble was when I was with a group of friends; I would try to get them to move faster. Since they knew why I wanted them to move faster, they would purposely go slower so the girls could catch up with us. They used to get a kick out of it when the girls would drive me crazy. One day, I was so afraid when I saw the girls were ahead of us, and I did not want to catch with them, I pretended that my foot was hurting. I stopped and pulled one shoe off, and I used a rock and started hitting on the shoe like a nail was bothering me in the shoe. Then I started to limp a few steps to let the other guys go ahead of me. It did not work, because the girls found out that I was behind them, so they waited until we caught up with them.

That particular day, they began to scream: *P'tit Joel Cuff Moulin Hooray! P'tit Joel Cuff Moulin. Hooray! P'tit Joel Cuff Moulin, Hooray!* I could not feel my legs, and my heart was beating so hard that I thought that I was going to suffer a heart attack. I don't know how I survived the afternoon. When I got home, I explained the situation to my brother Jarman. He told me that he was coming with meet me the next day and that we should try to meet with the girls so he could straighten them out. I did not know what was going to happen. The following day, I did what my brother asked me to do. I was so determined to meet with the girls that I left the school early that day. I ran to a neutral place where I met with Jarman, and we waited for them.

Of course, when they saw me they began to scream: *P'tit Joel Cuff Moulin Hooray! P'tit Joel Cuff Moulin"Hooray! "P'tit Joel Cuff Moulin" Hooray!*

I had no fear because Jarman was there. Jarman and I made a complete stop, so they could meet with us. Jarman asked one of the girls, "Who is the leader of the group?"

She answered, "Why do you want to know?"

Jarman said, "I would like to tell this person to stop bothering my brother or someone is going to get hurt."

They started to laugh and started to scream: *P'tit Joel Cuff Moulin Hooray! P'tit Joel Cuff Moulin Hooray! P'tit Joel Cuff Moulin Hooray!*

What they did not know was that I had already told Jarman who the leader was. Suddenly, Jarman walked toward the leader and slapped her so hard that she fell on the ground. Then he kicked two more girls in the group. I took the opportunity to beat up a few of them for what they did to me in the past. From then on, I was able to live a normal school life. Ironically, Jarman and I both in the following years went out with two of the girls.

The year 1963 was a year of adversities; it was the year that my family would have a brush with death, and our lives would be drastically changed. It began in June. I was ten and happy, even though I was still sleeping in the church. As I mentioned before, there were two rooms in the home where we all lived. There was Mom, Dad, Giscelaine, Ruth, Marie France, Marie Nicole, the maid Melina, and a little girl *(Restavec)* named Odette who was helping Melina. That was already too many for the "crib."

A young man, Antonio, who was living with the family as a *Jardinier* (gardener), my brother Jarman, and I had to sleep in the church. The church did not have any doors, and the windows were made with a kind of specially designed blocks that had a lot of holes to allow light and wind to pass through. We would use the church benches to block the front door, the side door, and the windows while we slept. Most of the time, we would gather together in front of the house each afternoon until late night.

As a way of transportation, there were a number of big buses that carried passengers from Port-au-Prince to Cayes, the third largest city of the country. There were also other forms of transportation such as trawlers and small vans. In Port-au-Prince, there was a major bus and trawler station where people came every morning to catch buses or trawlers to go around the country. The buses were the luxurious and expensive rides, while the trawlers were less comfortable and cheaper. Since we were living in the South, the buses and the trawlers would leave in the morning from Port-au-Prince to Cayes and return from the Cayes to Port-au-Prince the following morning. That simply meant they would pass in front of our house in the afternoon going to Cayes, and in the morning going to Port-au-Prince. Even though the distance from the two cities was approximately 125 miles, the buses could only make one, one-way trip per day. Those that traveled to the west passed by in the morning, and those that traveled to the south passed by in the afternoon. They were not like the Greyhound buses or like the trawlers that we have in the U.S., but they were still well designed and pretty. Each one would have a name and a few short quotes or proverbs, but the names would be in the top front of them, not like the busses we have here in the states. Some of the names were *La Sagesse* (Sage or Wise), *Fleur De Mai* (May Flower), *Sainte Rose de Lima* (St. Rose de Lima), *La Diligeance* (Diligence), and *L'Aurore* (Dawn), to name a few.

In our neighborhood, we were among the few who could speak French. We sat in the front porch, or *la galerie,* watching buses and trawlers passing along. Every time one passed, we called its name out loud. At night, we sat around singing and cracking jokes. One night, a gentleman by the name of Altinor, who could not speak French, wanted to crack a joke in French, because we were joking in French.

He said, *Le noir dit le rouge, 'si mon tchou est creve, vous etes mort.'* The formal French translation would be *Le Noir dit a le Rouge, 'Si je suis troue, tu es mor.'* "The Black told the Red, 'If I have a hole in my bottom, you are dead.'"

It may not be funny for you, but it was for us. So we asked him what the meaning of his joke was. He said, *"Chaudière"* (a burned pot). I had one of the best summers a child could ever have that year, and without knowing, I was about to have the worst fall in my life. We were going to get hit by one of the worst hurricanes that ever hit Central America, more precisely the Western hemisphere, and probably never again. The name of the hurricane was "Flora."

The whole catastrophe began on the morning of October 10, 1963. It was drizzling and the sun would not come out. Most people did their normal errands, because it was not raining hard. Around 3 p.m., it started to get dark and the rain got heavier. The wind started to pick up speed. I don't believe that we had a radio at home, so we did not know what to expect. Around six o'clock, it started pouring, and we could see the trees, banana, coconut, and others began to twist. It got darker, and the rain and the wind were coming and passing with rage. The next hour, Dad told us that we were under attack by a cyclone and that it was going to a big one. Everyone got inside that little house. At that time, we were in the process of adding two more rooms to the house. God always works miracles. Because the walls were attached to the existing house, that strengthened it. The roof on the expansion was not installed yet. By 8 p.m., we began to experience the real ordeal. It was just like a bulldozer moving back and forth against the house. It was so bad that Nicole, my baby sister, (at that time, she was about five years old) asked Dad if we were in hell and the devils were destroying us. We were asked to stay in one spot to pray to the Lord for forgiveness, asking him to have mercy on our souls because we really thought that we were going to die. At one point, the entire roof of the house was blown away. If you remember the catastrophic Hurricane Katrina, which terrified the state of Louisiana in the year of 2005, other than the resulting flood, the incident that I am trying to describe here was far worse. We could hear the whistle of the sheet metal flying off a number of houses that were covered with sheet metals.

The hurricane lasted for a good three or four hours, which felt like an eternity. God protected us. We all survived the ordeal with a few scratches. *"Be strong and courageous. Do not be afraid or terrified because of them for the Lord your God goes with you. He will never leave you nor forsake you" (Deuteronomy 31:6, NIV).* One of my brothers, Robert, was visiting a friend. He could not make it back home, but he was also safe. Nevertheless, we thought he was dead, but the same God who protected us was there for him as well. Not only did Robert survive the monster, but he recognized that he was saved miraculously, for he was somewhat buried under a pile of wreckages and debris. He made a promise to God. He asked God to give him a second chance, to let him live, and he would give the rest of his life to faithfully serve Him and be a "Porte-Parole" across the globe, speaking about the greatness of His Son Jesus Christ. Robert kept his promise, and guess what.

His first born, Robert Serge, Jr., is an ordained pastor as well. The next day was clear, and the sky was blue, but there was no sign of the sun. Now, I think the reason why it was so bright was because there were no trees, and all houses were completely destroyed. Everyone was sad and silent; I believe we were in a state of shock. People were looking for other loved ones or friends, wondering whether they were dead or alive, hurt or unhurt. The street turned to a river. You could stand anywhere and look at anything that stood about miles away. The wind hit the area at 120 mph, killing five thousand people. There were more than fifty-seven inches of rain and a twelve-foot storm surge. The heavy rains and gale force winds damaged and destroyed, as I said above, houses, crops, livestock, and properties. The storm disrupted all communication wires.

We lost everything that we owned. I mean everything: shoes, clothes, pictures, furniture, which was not that much to begin with. We were very sad, but felt very fortunate to be alive. I walked in the street up and down to see if my friends were still alive. Thank God, none of them got killed. One of my dad's friends died, decapitated by flying sheet metal. The next six years in my life would be turned upside down. My two oldest sisters would get married in the following years. Ironically, my first nephew would be born from my first sister, who was seventeen years old, on the same day of another deadly hurricane, Inez. My second sister, Ruth, had a son who died at two years old. I still can remember how sad we all were.

Growing up, I was the black sheep of the family and the one who got more whippings than the other kids. I did a lot of stupid things at that time. One night my dad was having a church service. I took one of my sisters' clothes, and I dressed like a lady. I used a handkerchief and wrapped it around my head. I entered the church and sat in the rear. As I mentioned before, the church did not have doors, and it did not have electricity as well. This is to say that there were no lights. God always provides. Where most people were using oil lamps, we were blessed to have "Cole-man Lanterns" The sanctuary was not well lit and besides, the Coleman was positioned towards the front areas. My dad spotted a stranger in the assembly, and of course, he wanted to welcome the visitor.

Dad said, "Ha! We have a visitor here with us tonight. Praise the Lord. I would like to make time for the visitor to introduce herself."

I did not say anything.

Dad said, "Madame, you don't have to be shy. This is the church of God. We are one in the love of Jesus."

The people in the church were waiting to hear the visitor. At that moment, I got up as if I were going to say something, but instead I stood and moved toward the closest door, when suddenly, my dad said, "Hold it right there, mister."

I stopped. Dad asked one of the deacons to sing a song, and he stepped down from the pulpit walking toward me. He grabbed me by the arm and dragged me out of the church; there I was administered "une fessée" (a whipping). Another time, while my dad was having a church service, I decided to do something freaky. I tied several men together through their belt loops without their knowledge. My father's church was very primitive; men sat on one side and women on the other side. So it was not too much of a problem to take care of my business. After I got a complete row of brothers, I moved to the next row and patiently did the same, one by one, threading a string through the loops. Then I waited quietly for dad to ask the congregation to stand. Of course, minutes later Dad stood behind the pulpit and announced that the Scripture of the day would be read in such and such book of the Bible, and the magic words came up: "Please stand." You can imagine what happened. It was like a domino effect. The whole church full of people was laughing so hard that Dad had to call for order.

It did not take too long for Dad to figure out what happened. He announced in a loud voice, "P'tit Joel, I am going to take away the devil out of you, mister." That day my *derrière* was totaled. Dad cut it like a wild grass.

In most places in Haiti and especially in the provinces, when someone dies, the whole family cries loudly in horrible and lamentable ways. Anyone could hear their voices far away. That is the way you know where and when someone dies. Every time I would hear those screams, I would go out to find the house where that person had passed. Guess what! It was just for one thing—"A few cups of coffee with breads." The stupid thing was, after drinking so much coffee, I realized how far I had to walk to get there. I had some difficulties getting back home, because most of the time, it would take me hours of walking to find the places. Ironically, that did not stop me from going to the next bereaved family's home.

In 1967/1968, I was fourteen or fifteen years old. I remember that Dad was sick and hospitalized for a long time. During that time, Mom made several trips in a month back and forth to and from Port-au-Prince. Mom would take one of us with her to see Dad on each trip. In one particular month, it was my turn to go with Mom. By then, I was a real hillbilly. I was so happy to get the opportunity to go back to Port-au-Prince. I had a major problem. I did not have a pair of shoes to wear. I had to borrow a pair from my brother Jarman.

There is no way that I can explain my joy and the emotion when I arrived in Port-au-Prince. The lights, the cars, the streets, the way people dressed, I could not control myself. It was like paradise. I could not wait to go back home so I could tell my relatives and my friends what I saw. As I said earlier, to go to Port-au-Prince was not too much of a problem, because the buses passed right in front of the house. We would flag them down to check for seat availability. Those that did not have seats available would not stop. Sometimes, we would stop them on their way going south to reserve a seat for the next day's travel. Coming home from the west was totally different. We would have to go to the bus station very early in the morning in order to get good seats. There we would wait until the bus was full, which could take anywhere from three to five hours. Then the bus would leave the station to begin the journey. A typical trip, from waiting in the station to arriving at home, would take eight or nine hours. No one made a big deal of it, because going to Port-au-Prince was a privilege for many people.

The academic school year of 1969–970 was my last year in Miragoâne. I was sixteen going on seventeen. That year was my best one, not because I had my first girlfriend, but because I was going to begin my secondary school. And that was going to be the end of going to school every other year.

My first girlfriend, (kiddy love) whom I will call Deedee to protect her identity, was born to unsaved parents, and she was not saved either. She was a very nice girl. She would come to Miragoâne from Port-au-Prince every summer to spend time with her parents. Her parents were divorced. She lived in Port-au-Prince with her father's relatives, but both of her parents lived in Miragoâne. However, when she was visiting, she stayed over at her Dad's house. Her dad owned a lot of businesses. Their house was approximately three miles from mine. I would walk to her house every afternoon to spend fifteen to twenty minutes with her in front of her house, just to talk. To begin with, I was not allowed to enter her house. At the end, she became a Christian and a good one. She got baptized by my Dad in his church. The following year, she did not want to go out with me any longer, because I was slacking off. When I began my secondary school, I was wild and stupid; I would not behave as a Christian. I tried in vain to reconcile with her. As I am writing this book, Deedee is happily married to her husband of about twenty-five years, and coincidently, her husband is also a PK (Preacher's Kid), and she remains a good Christian. I got reconnected with her after twenty-eight years; I also met her husband, a great guy and a very educated man. We are respectfully good friends. I think God put me in Deedee's path for a brief time so she could be saved.

A couple of things happened during the final year of school in Miragoâne. Every student, at the end of his primary year of school, must take a national test exam. That exam lasted three days, usually Monday, Tuesday, and Wednesday. Most students, if not all, wore brand new clothes. My folks, unfortunately, did not have money to buy new clothes for me. My Mom had a new skirt. She took it apart and used the material to make two shirts of different styles for me. Not only were they beautiful, but also the sentiment attached to them had a strong effect on me. I took the national exam and I passed it. Eventually, I was granted a certificate.

Something else happened. I needed to go to Port-au-Prince to take an exam that would qualify me to enter the secondary school. The same kind of thing happened again; I did not have a pair of shoes to wear. That time I borrowed a pair shoes from a member of my father's church, Pastor Avelant Pierre, who had just graduated from a Bible school and gotten accepted to be an evangelist in Dad's church. I am very grateful to him to this day. I made the fabulous trip to Port-au-Prince thinking that I was coming back to Miragoâne to say my final goodbye and to return the shoes, but I ended up staying in Port-au-Prince. Oh! By the way, I did send the shoes back to Brother Avelant. Thirty years later, in one of my many trips to Haiti, I reconnected with Brother Avelant in a church service. Of course, what came into my mind was the pair of shoes, which made me look at his feet. He was wearing a pair of shoes that were so bad, that he would have been better walk barefoot. At that time, I wore a brand new pair of "Mezland" shoes. I pulled him aside and thanked him for the time that he let me use his shoes to go the Port-au-Prince for my secondary education entrance exam. He did not believe that happened, and told me that I confused him for someone else. I gave him money to buy a pair of shoes. I am not going into detail now, but later on, I felt that I should give him the shoes that I wore. Hopefully, I will have the chance to write and talk about my true feelings regarding the shoes issue. In Port-au-Prince, I would enter a third phase of my life.

SEVENTEEN YEARS OLD TO TWENTY-THREE YEARS OLD

Life in Port-au-Prince

At Port-au-Prince, I was supposed to go over to my godfather's house. First let me tell you about him. My godfather, who was also my adopted father, was married to my biological father's sister. His name was Jean Noël Tingue. He was born on December 25, 1927, and died on December 25, 2008, on his birthday. Because of this birth date, his parents called him Noel and because of me, everyone, including his biological children, called him Père Noël. Père Noël loved me unconditionally from the time I was in my Mom's womb. He told my parents that he would want to be my godfather, and if I were to be a boy, he would want to adopt me. After he made it clear to my folks, he began to take care of my Mom while she was carrying me. And after I was born, he continued to care for me. I spent most of my vacation time and weekends over at his house until my parents moved us to Miragoâne. Père Noël has seven biological children: Edith, Guilaine, Renel, Mirèille, Madone, Nicole, and Ninon. Now you can see why he wanted to adopt me. So God heard his prayer. This chapter is the most difficult one for me to write, and I have already written it twice. You will understand the reason why later. I promise you. It is very difficult for me not to think or believe that Père Noël was not my biological Dad. As I said above you will see later the love that I was to know and receive from him and the whole family. I was going to be his favorite child.

My brother Jarman and I came to Port-au-Prince together to continue our education. As I mentioned before, I was to stay over at Père Noël's house, and Jarman was to stay over at Aunt Clerciné Michel's house. Mrs. Clerciné Michel was my biological Dad's oldest sister. Ordinarily, my parents would have brought us to these folks' homes and placed us under their care. Oh, no! It did not happen like that. We came by ourselves. I was afraid to separate myself from Jarman. So I did not want to go to Père Noël's home, but we were going there every day to eat. Let me back up a little. The week that we arrived in Port-au-Prince, we met with a few other cousins who asked us where we were going to stay. We told them that Jarman was to stay at Mrs. Michel's house, and I at Pere Noel's.

They told us that Père Noël was very strict, and when he put a "whoop" on you, only Jesus can save you from him. That was scary, because I thought that when I left Miragoâne, I was through with *Bâton (whipping.)* In spite of that, we continued to go there. One day while we were walking up the street to go in the house, we heard a funny noise, like someone was getting beat up. I am telling you, it was like the worst criminal in town was being whipped. Next thing we saw, one of the girls was getting whipped by Père Noël. Jarman and I ran like chickens. I definitely decided that I was not going there. So we stayed at

Aunt Clerciné's house. Over at Père Noël's house, the food was always served formally—banana, meat, rice, and bean sauce. While at my aunt's home, most of the time, we would get a plate to share. After two weeks, we decided to go back to Père Noël's to eat. That particular night, Père Noël made it clear to me that I did not have two chances. I was to stay or not to come back. I chose to stay. I went over to my aunt's house to pick up my few pieces of clothing that I had, and went back to Père Noël's for good. It was about the end of August or beginning of September. The third phase of my life began the very next day.

That night I slept on a twin bed with my brother Renel. Picture in your mind two young men, age seventeen, sleeping in that small bed. We had to sleep *Tèt nan pié et pié nan tèt*. Translation: we slept in the opposite directions, head to toe.

My first morning, Renel and I woke up, and he said to me, "Let's go outside to wash up." I said okay. Even though we lived in Port-au-Prince, we did not have any modern comfort in the house. We had to wash up and do *doudou* outside. Renel washed his face and started to brush his teeth. He stopped for a minute and asked me where my toothbrush was. I told him that I did not have one. It may sound sick or unhealthy, but please try to see the meaning of his gesture. Renel finished brushing his teeth. He rinsed the brush, handed it to me, and told me to brush my teeth. That was the first time that I brushed my teeth with a toothbrush in years. That was a way for him to tell me that I was a brother and that he felt very comfortable with me. Renel and I were going to live like that for as long as I was going to be in Haiti. Still today, when he lived in Montreal and I in the U.S., we are much closer. Père Noël brought me a toothbrush the same day. I did not have to use my brother's toothbrush anymore.

At seventeen years old, I was nothing but a classic hillbilly young man. My pants were all "high-water." I did not have a good pair of shoes, my shirts were all too small for me, and I talked like an outer-city boy. The dilemma was that we were to go to school with a group of city young men who were Renel's friends. I was four years behind the regular grade that I should be in. In Miragoâne, because there were so many of us, we would take turns going to school. Those who attended school the previous year would stay home while the others attend the following year. So I was more likely in seventh grade at age seventeen.

Most of the time, we walked to school, spent the day, and walked back in the afternoon. The guys, Renel's friends, talked badly about my appearance and the way I walked around. I slowed them down, because I was looking around for cars, big buildings, interesting looking people, and other things that I did not see in Miragoâne. The guys told Renel to hold my hand, otherwise I would get lost. They said it in a way that I could hear, and they were laughing so hard that Renel would get upset. I wish I could have told Renel that I loved him so much for putting up with those jerks. I never felt that I was an embarrassment for Renel or that he was embarrassed by me. He always showed me agape love. Those other guys would treat me that badly for the whole school year.

Please keep this in mind. Those same guys would later be at my mercy for a lot of things. I was going to be their mentor. I was going to be the first guy to work and make big money in the group. I was going to have more girlfriends and be the first to have a car. Not only did I not fit in with their lifestyle, but I was far behind those guys in school. I was very embarrassed to be in the classroom with a bunch of twelve and thirteen-year-old kids. That situation was going to force me to do something that no one that I knew had ever done. I was going to skip every other grade until graduation. In Haiti at that time, it took seven years to complete secondary school. The final grade is like the freshman year in college. At the completion of the secondary school, one would be ready to enter the university. Most people start working after completion of secondary school, especially those who could not enter the universities.

At that time there were four major universities, all state operated: the University of Medicine, of Agriculture, of Law, and of Engineering. It was, and probably still is, extremely difficult to be admitted to any of them. One would need to have the following factors to get a chance of getting in: government sponsorship, which means you have to have a high-ranked personage in the Haitian military, a dad who is a doctor, lawyer, engineer, or an agronomist, and/or you could only get into the university that your parents had attended. There were a few trade schools that taught such subjects as welding, auto mechanics, and carpentry. Unfortunately, the students that had completed their secondary school would have some difficulties attending trade schools, because trade schools, at that time, were for dropped out students. They thought those kinds of schools were beneath them.

My brother Paul left the country at the end of 1970 and went to the island of Guadeloupe. From there, he went to Martinique and later on to the Unites States, New York to be precise. I had a fun Christmas in 1970. I spent the night in a *Réveiiions,* a common name use for Christmas parties in Haiti. I also spent a lot of time studying my brother Renel's friends, who at that time became also my friends. I tried to detect their weaknesses, things that they did properly and did not. As I said earlier, they were far more advanced than I in many ways: academically, economically, and intellectually. So that was my first challenge to conquer.

In Miragoâne, I was a street fighter. I would do anything to pick a fight with someone, and usually, someone who was bigger than me. The reason was simple. If I got beat, I could always say, "The guy is much bigger than I am. That is why I lost the fight." But by winning a few fights, I would also win some respect. Indeed, my plan worked. The guys began to feel more comfortable with me, because when I was with them, they felt they were protected.

In January 1971, the president of Haïti, François Duvalier (Papa Doc), was giving a national speech on one of the National

Palace's porches. There were thousands of people on the front lawn and the street. All schools were invited to come. Our school, a public school, had a marching band. I was in one group of students that was giving an exhibition called *Corps D'honneur du Lycée Alexandre Pétion.* We were to perform in front of the palace on the main lawn.

That particular day, I decided to enter the palace to meet with the president. Most of the students in our unit and I proceeded toward the main door. I knew for sure that I was somewhere inside of the palace and that I was going up the stairs. Next thing I knew, I was on my back on the lawn, very close to where I started. Some of the students were laughing at me. As of this day, I do not know how I got out there on my back. Ironically, after eighteen years, I would sit, eat, and party in the national palace.

Speaking of irony, eighteen years later, I was in the presidential palace in the office of one of my brothers-in law, my wife's brother, who was at that time an army captain and head of the president's security service, when he asked a lieutenant to go over the project manager's office to get something for him. The project manager was also my brother-in-law, my sister's husband. The lieutenant told him that he did not know where the office of the project manager was in the palace. I told the lieutenant, "I am going to show you where it is." Please note: The lieutenant was a presidential guard palace officer.

I successfully completed the academic year 1971 -1972, and I was going to skip the following grade. Since they would not let me skip a grade in the same school, I left the school and went to another school, *Lycée Anthenor Firmin,* to pursue the third year of the seven-year period.

By now, I was getting accepted almost everywhere. I realized that the guys (our friends) did not know how to slow dance. So I learned how to slow dance without letting them know. French is the official language of the country, and Creole is the mother tongue. It was not then, nor now, a matter of official language. If you are not brought up in an elite family where French is the family language, you are going to have some difficulties maintaining a fluent French conversation. In order to make a good impression on a girl, one should be able to speak French without toil, so I made it a priority to converse in French at all times. Once again it worked. I was the best dancer and the best-spoken guy of all my friends. By Christmas 1971, I had my first official girlfriend, Marie Danienne, a beautiful girl who lived across the street.

In the spring of 1972, I would adopt a nickname, "Roc." I was going to get that name for the number of fights that I was going to pick in classrooms while waiting for the next teacher to come, or when the next teacher failed to show up. During that time and for the next few years, when we needed some money from Dad, my brother Renel and I would wait for hours in front of *Bazaar Au Lincoln*, where the "Tap Taps" (small buses/taxies) would go through on their way in and out of Petion-ville. My Dad, Père Noël, used to own one of those Tap Taps, so he would give us a couple dollars or less depending on the day. With that money we had a ball, and we could easily have a shopping spree. Again I completed the school year with no sweat. I did the same thing I did before. I left that school and registered myself in another school. I took their exams and passed by a wide margin. Yes, I mean I skipped the next grade and went on to the grade above.

It took a lot of discipline and determination to do what I did. Frank Gant wrote: "Happy are those who dream dreams and are ready to pay the price to make them come true." Throughout my life, I have been and will be ready to pay any price to make my dreams come true. I have always refused to believe that I could not do something and always refused to pass up any opportunity offered to me. I always wanted to advance and learn new things. I often had to press on my way to prove a point or to get an opportunity, but this was not the case with school. My goals were to finish the secondary school a year after the guys, and to become a lawyer. Unfortunately, I was going to fail to accomplish both. Why? The national education personnel would not let me take the national and final exam, not because I would not be qualified or ready, but because I skipped the grade before. There was a new law which went into effect the same year that I was supposed to take the test, and I would not get admitted in the university without passing successfully the national exam.

Anyway, up to that point, I was having a great life. Three of my biological brothers, one sister, and my mom were living and working in the U.S. They were sending *beaucoup d'argent* for the rest of us in Haïti. It has been a pattern, or may I say a way of life, for Haitian immigrants to support the families that they left behind. Besides money, they also will help bring them to the U.S., or the country they immigrated to. As life is getting tougher in Haiti, Haitians living outside of Haïti continue to send more money there. I read an article by Guyler Delva, Haitian Times, 7 March 2007. I paraphrase: *Haïtians sent over 1 to 1.5 billion dollars to their families in Haïti per year. The majority of that cash came from USA.* As Haitian immigrants, my family did not want us to have financial problems. In Port-au-Prince, in the beginning, things were tough; I learned how to swim with the sharks. I also lived large and enjoyed my youth to the fullest. I tried to outsmart all my friends, especially to get more girls: two, three girlfriends at once. I know it sounds sick, but it is the truth. I thought that I was the king of the jungle. Basically, I was treated like one by my family and my friends. I love my family. I was treated with so much love, especially by Père Noël.

I enjoyed many adventures in Port-au-Prince. Remember that I said I did not want to go over to Père Noël's house because of the whipping he had administered to one of my sisters. I had witnessed a few more with my brother Jarman. Why do I say that? It is to set the tone for the event that I am about to explain. On a Sunday afternoon, Jarman came to pick me up on a motorcycle, but he left it down the street, because he did not want Père Noël to see it. I left with Jarman. We went to a city about eight miles from my house. On our way back, we had an accident. While we were crossing a railroad, the bike slid, and we fell right in the middle of the street. Something was strange. Jarman got up and I could not. That was when I realized my foot was trapped between the motorcycle's chain and the back tire. Jarman and I managed to remove the foot from where it was caught. My heel was cut deeply. We were so shocked, we did not know what to do. A passerby stopped and helped us out by providing transportation to the hospital. I was going to the hospital, but there weren't any doctors to take care of me.

On that particular Sunday, there was the most magnificent soccer game in the history of Haïti. The king of soccer, Pélé, was playing that day. So every single doctor and resident was at the game. There I was lying in a hospital bed, waiting to receive some care, and the caregivers were all off having fun at the game. The accident occurred at about 4:00 p.m., and I was in the hospital till 4 a.m. on Monday morning. After I got in the hospital, I told Jarman to go home and to tell Père Noël about the accident. Jarman, who was so afraid of Père Noël, did not go to the house. He went to the neighborhood and asked someone there to deliver the news, and left right away before Père Noël could see him.

When my family received the news, it was already 10 p.m. Everyone was upset. My sister Edith, who was in her fourth year of medical school, came in and began to administer first aid to my foot while waiting for some doctors to come back from the game. Besides the cut on my heel, my leg was dislocated in three areas: the ankle, the knee, and the upper leg area. The accident was one of the signs to prove that I was truly loved by everyone in the Tingue's family, but later on their love for me would manifest much more. I never blamed Jarman for not wanting to go to announce the accident for fear that Père Noël would yell at him or even whip his *derrière*. Another day, Père Noël decided to whip Mirièlle's *derrière*, but something went wrong. Mirièlle, who was about fifteen or sixteen years, tried to reason with him, and he got upset. He jumped on her. That time he was using his bare hand to hit her. He threw a punch at her and missed. His hand struck a headboard made of iron. Suddenly, he stopped screaming and took a weird look around like he had heard God's voice telling him not to strike the girl no more. He went to the next room and sat down for a minute. Then he called me to come see him. He asked me to go with him to the hospital and also asked not to say anything to anyone.

Unfortunately, that day there was no car available, so we began to walk down the street to the main road to catch a taxi. Still, he did not say why we were going to the hospital. When we got to the main road, it was apparent that something was wrong with Père Noël, but I was afraid to ask what it was. Père Noël in a poor voice said to me, "That stupid girl made me break my arm."

I asked, "How do you know that it broke?" He did not answer the question. "Dammit!" he exclaimed. Then he asked, "What am I going to tell everybody?"

It was not a question to answer, so I did not respond. We took a taxi to drop us at the hospital. Yes indeed, his arm was broken in two places. Can you imagine if he had struck Mirièlle's head what could have happened? When we got back home, it seemed that everyone was already aware that his arm was broken. So Père Noël was very embarrassed, and since that time, I don't recall him ever hitting any of us ever again. I have to admit that Père Noël never whipped my *derrière*. By the way, Père Noël told all his friends that his hand got caught in the steering wheel of his car and that broke his arm.

Sharing was always my passion. I never wanted to see someone lacking of what I had or could have. This is a trait that I grew up with and have even today. I enjoy helping others. The difference between now and then is that I think first before acting and try to maintain a level of ethnicity.

I gave an old pair of shoes that Père Noël had under the bed to a gentleman who used to wash Père Noël's car at lunchtime. In Haiti, for clarification, most people kept their shoes under their beds. Only people from the upper class and the elites have closets. Père Noël, who had not used the shoes for almost a year, decided to wear them after the fact. Of course, he could not find them. He did not mind too much because, like I said, they were old. That poor guy, the car washer, whose name is Fenel, was so happy that I gave him a pair of shoes, he chose me to be the godfather of his son. Fenel wore the shoes on the day of the baptism. Père Noël noticed them and began to tell everyone that Fenel stole his shoes.

"How dare he?" Père Noël said. And he was about to confront Fenel, when one of my siblings came and told me. I apologized to Père Noël for the fact that I gave his shoes to Fenel. I did the same thing to my brother Renel, but that time it was a shirt. Actually, Renel saw someone else wearing the shirt, and he automatically asked the guy to take it off right on the street and give it to him. I was not happy at all, because Renel and I wore the same clothes. I mean after they were washed and ironed. That is to say, that shirt also belonged to me.

My last attempt to pick a fight was going to be a lesson learned for the rest of my life. One night, I sat on a porch of an old girlfriend's house. The girl was the niece of a voodoo priestess who was married to a voodoo priest. I don't know what was going through my mind, because as a "PK" (preacher's kid), I had no business being in love with that girl.

Blessed is the man who does not walk in the counsel of the wicked or stand in the way of sinners or sit in the seat of mockers. But his delight is in the law of the Lord, and on his law he meditates day and night. (Psalm, 1:1- 2)

I knew I should not be there, but throughout the book, you will see that God wanted me to live to fulfill the purpose. Ironically, while I was sitting there, a few gentlemen were passing by and were ridiculing someone. They were saying, "Dirty Voodoo Priest, go away. You are the son of the devil." Then they called someone, who I'll call "Romeo," a vagabond. I change his name, and I will change the names of the following characters to protect their identities. When I heard that name, everything changed because of whom the gentlemen were ridiculing. Romeo was the uncle of my girlfriend and the father of a very good friend of Renel and me, who I will call Joe. Joe was inside of the house; he also heard those guys ridiculing his dad. Joe decided to go after them for a combative confrontation. Joe's mom did not want her son to get hurt and asked me to go after him, so I could stop him from doing anything stupid. I agreed to go, even though I did not like the fact that I was going to get involved in a fight with someone who was against the voodooist. The guys ran down the pathways to go into the street where there were plenty of lights. I went up there, and I saw Joe arguing with two gentlemen. One was about five feet and seven inches, 165 pounds, and the other one was about five feet, 130 pounds. I was very reluctant to confront them, simply because I was a pastor's kid. it was not the right thing to do. Period!

My girlfriend was coming behind me, and she saw that her cousin was in a heated confrontation with the guys. So she asked me to intervene. Forcefully, I went to the shorter and slimmer guy. I told him that I would not fight him, because he was not my size. Therefore, I lightly touched his shoulder as if I wanted to push him away. He said, "Man, I am a Christian. I don't like voodoo priests. And besides, yes, I am too small to fight." Now, I lightly pushed him aside. Then I turned to the other one. I asked him if he wanted to fight me. He gave me almost the same answer. I stepped away. Next thing I knew, Joe pulled a jumbo army knife from his pocket, and he jumped on the bigger guy.

The smaller guy automatically drew a jumbo revolver and told Joe, "If you hurt him I will shoot you point blank." He wasn't kidding, because he cocked his revolver. When Joe, who was well known in the area, got involved, few people stepped in to stop the drama. So the slim guy now got angry and demanded that Joe be arrested, and he asked where I was. When I heard him ask that, I hid myself behind a tree so I could still see what was happening. Unfortunately, no one could do anything for Joe, because the gentleman not only had a mega-revolver, but he also had a lot of power. This is to say that Joe was arrested. I found out that the gunman was a brutal detective and hitman in the city. According to a few people who knew him, he would not have taken a second to think about it. He would have shot both of us in the blink of an eye. Oh! By the way, Joe spent the night in jail. Yes, that was the end of my street-fighting era.

During the summer of 1973, Jarman came to see me with a gentleman he introduced to Renel and me as Pierre Gerard Mirbel. Reverend Mirbel, Jarman's friend, remains our close friend to this day. He is like a brother to me. I call him Pastor Pierre, a great man. That afternoon of our first meeting, Jarman told me that Pierre had just bought a car, but he did not know how to drive. So Jarman came to pick me up to drive the car to Pierre's house. I did not know how to drive either, but Jarman had no doubt that I was the best driver in the city, even though he had never seen me behind a wheel. Those days, I would tell everybody that I knew how to do everything and anything. You think I would let the guys think that I did not know how to drive? Oh, heck no!

Instead, I said, "Let's go, gentlemen." We took a Tap Tap to drop us where the car was. It was a white, stick shift Opel. I got in the car. Pierre sat in the front passenger side; Renel and Jarman sat in the back. The moment of truth was about to be revealed. I started the car and tried to take off. Every time I lifted my foot off the clutch, the car would die. So I asked the guys to get out and push the car, and I told them that the car had an alternator problem. Since it was such a small car, between starting and pushing, we managed to take it over to Pierre's house. Even Renel, who lived in the same house and who was always with me, thought I knew how to drive.

Four years after, I would take a greater chance by driving a car. This time it would be a company car, and I would get severely embarrassed and humiliated. Hang on! I have done a lot of things that were not right, but my intentions were always to survive. I thought that time was passing me by, and I wanted to prove to my friends that even though I did not have the same opportunities than they had, I could compete with them and even bit them in their own games. So I bluffed my way to the front, and at the end, I would always win. If I had someone to coach or mentor me, I would have better foundation, and I would be doing much better without foil. I have no regrets; besides, I really think my life would not be so interesting. I survived a lot of obstacles in this life. First, I give thanks to God. Secondly, thanks to the people who threw me a few lifelines. And thirdly, thanks to my audacity. A good piece of advice: *The intelligent man learns from his mistakes, the wise man learns from others' mistakes.* Beware!

Once again, at the end of 1973, I successfully completed the academic year, and I left the Lycée to attend a private college, *College Honoré Ferry,* in order to gain more confidence for the next grade. That time, I did not skip a grade, because it was the introduction to the humanitarian grade level. That grade was one of the most important grades in the secondary school. My plan was to skip the following grade to go to the first grade, which was the class of Rhetoric, where all students have to take a five-day long national exam in order to go to the final grade, Philosophy. In Philosophy, all students would also have to undergo another five-day long exam. Students must be able to successfully complete the final exam to enter into universities. At that time, things were not bad for me. I was constantly receiving money, clothes, and shoes from the U.S., and I was pretty much at the same level as the other guys, but still not academically equal to them. I had several girlfriends in the area where I lived and the surrounding areas.

I began the year with pride and honor. Nevertheless, I would pay the price later. I would not be able to graduate, even though I would be academically sound. I'll explain. After com pleting the humanitarian grade, I left the school and enrolled myself in another private *"College Arountino P'tit -Celin"* to begin the Rhetorical grade. Unfortunately, the same year that I enrolled into the grade, there was a decree that students who did not complete the prior grade were not eligible to undergo the national exam. I had two choices: go back and do the prior grade, which would put me back two years, or audit the final grade, *"Faire la Philo libre,"* an expression that we often use in Haiti. Well, I somehow accomplished a great portion of my goal. Not being able to graduate did not bother me too much, because I knew that I was coming to the U.S., which was almost everyone's dream. Sometime down the road, I added one more girlfriend to the circle, Malie, who I decided to take out to a celebration party.

The party was about thirty-five miles south of Port-au-Prince. That sounds pretty close, but it took almost one and a half to two hours to get there. Anyway, Malie was already there for the weekend. I went there by bus. The famous *Coupé Clouré* orchestra, which means *cut and nailed,* was playing for the evening. That was one of my best nights out, but something was about to happen which would stay in my cousin Tony's mind, forever. Tony is an ordained minister at present. I picked up my girl at the place she stayed, and we went to the party. The admission fee was $10.00 per person. Believe it or not, that was a lot of money for a party out of town at that time. I bought tickets for my girl and myself. We went in there and found a table in a corner. The party began and we started to dance. While we were on the dance floor, we spotted my cousin Tony dancing with a girl that I will call Jessiline. Jessiline, whose parents lived right across from Malie's House, was a friend of my sister Ruth. She lived with other close family downtown. My sister Ruth liked her a lot and did not like Malie that much. Ruth always thought that Jessiline was too good for me and wanted to "hook" her up with Jarman, because he was always more serious than I, and Jarman always looked more mature and had a more impressive look. I checked with Tony and told him where I sat in case he would need me. Every half an hour to one hour, I would check with Tony.

What I did not tell you was that one of my brother in-law, André, who was not saved yet, and who was also in the party, paid the admission fee for Tony and Jessiline. Unfortunately, Tony did not have any money that day. So he was at the mercy of André. After a while, I did not check with Tony anymore, knowing that he was okay. So it was time to take Malie home. I left with her, with the intention of going back to the party to continue having fun. Upon my return to the party, I was looking for Tony. I asked André and his mate where Tony was. He told me that they did not know. I began to look for him. I looked all over the place; there was no sign of my Cousin. I proceeded to where the gates were. As I was getting closer to the gates, I heard a heated argument at the doorway. I cautiously moved toward the gates.

I heard a man who screamed loudly, *Ké tonè krazém, mouin andédan-an,* a common way to swear in Haiti, mostly by very mad people. It means, *If I were not in there, may a lightning bolt strike me.* Apparently the gatekeeper did not believe him, and he swore again.

At that time, I went closer to find out who was screaming so loudly. To my big surprise, it was my cousin Tony. I jumped on the gatekeeper's throat. I slapped him and I told him, "Pa jam bétizé ak figu moune dé-bien" which means *Don't you ever play game with a prestigious man's face.*

Then I took Tony inside. I always believed that it is not a question of size, strength, knowledge, but it was a question of will. As I said before, my brother was always bigger than I was and positively stronger, but my action was always greater. Inside of the party center, I asked him what the heck he was doing outside. He told me that he went to look for me. Sometime during the night, Jessiline asked him to buy some cigarettes for her. Since he didn't have any money, he asked André for some money to buy the cigarettes. At that time, one could buy three single cigarettes for 25 cents (Haitian) and the whole pack for 1 1/2 "Gourde." André, gave him 50 cents so he could buy six cigarettes for Jessiline. Sometime after, she asked him to buy her a beer. Tony went and asked André, for more money to buy a bottle of beer for Jessiline. At that time, André told him to "bug off." He felt so embarrassed; he did not say anything to her. He was trying to find me to get some cash. After he looked everywhere for me and did not see me, he thought that I was outside. That was why he went out without advising the gatekeeper that he was going out with the intention of coming back. The worst thing was Jessiline left the building and told them that she did not want to "mingle" with teenagers. That was a way to humiliate Tony. Ironically, I began to date Jessiline few months later. She was a lady with great appearance and personality. I had a lot of respect for her.

In that same neighborhood, there was an extremely pretty girl who lived a few houses down from Malie's house and right across from Ruth's house. Her name, to protect her identity, was Elsita. She was going out with a young fellow. She kind of looked like Toni Braxton. I used to be so upset when she would go out with the fellow. One day her boyfriend left the country for the U.S. I said, *"Béni soit l'Eternel"* (Praise the Lord.) I began my journey to win her heart. It took me almost a year, but I was happy to add her name to the noble circle at the end. During all of those fun days, I was able to complete my secondary education, but I could not apply to any university because I did not take either of the national final exams. At that time, those of my friends who successfully completed their secondary education and obtained their diplomas were able to go the university, and those who were not so fortunate had no choice but to gather together in the block to play a traditional poker game while every student and the working pals went to school and to work. On my first free year, I also began to play the traditional ten-cent poker game in the morning, but because I was always on a mission to improve myself, I attempted to filter my way to the *Université de Droit et des Sciences Economiques* (Law School), but it didn't work. I audited the first six months, and I gave up.

At that time my mom was living and working in the U.S. I wanted to prepare myself for a possible life in U.S. as well. One of the things that a foreigner needs to know in order to live in the U.S. is the language. I attended The Haitiano American Institute to learn the English language. I only took the introduction courses. While I was taking those English courses, my brother Renel, who had just completed a two-year program in a private engineering school studying topography, decided to study *La Comptabilité Française, chez Laroche,* French accounting at Laroche Institute. Well, I left my institute and accompanied him in the evening to his school where the professor did not mind me sitting in the classroom. I audited the entire program, but unlike Renel, I did not receive a certificate for the completion of the program.

At the beginning of 1977, a friend of the family, Marie France Dalencour, who was working for Hosking Western Sonderegger, an American company in Haiti, found that there was a need for a messenger. She told my dad, Père Noël, to send Renel for an interview. That company was to give technical help to a Haitian company that maintained the roads in Haïti. The Haitian company's name was *(SEPRRN) Service D'Entretien Permanent Du Réseau Routier National* (Service Permanent to Maintain the National Roads). The requirements for the position were: Applicant should be a bookkeeper or have a good knowledge of accounting, be able to communicate very well in English, and know how to drive and have a valid driver's license. Renel, who had a bookkeeper certificate, but did not know how to drive or how to speak English, was automatically ruled out. We had hoped that this job would be the ticket for a new life for the entire family. Needless to say, the family was very disappointed and sad to know that Renel was not qualified for the job. I was about to make a statement that would shock the family. I also was about to bite off something that I was going to have some tough times trying to swallow.

Remember that Jarman came to pick me up to drive a car home for Pierre, which I managed to do, and I had taken a couple of English courses. I don't have to remind you that I had a notion of accounting. You have an idea of what I am about to say. I called Père Noël and I told him, *"Pou kisa ou pa rekommandé-m pou travay-la?"* (Why don't you recommend me for the job?)

He said, *"Ti Tio, ou pa trop fò ni nan Kondui é nan palé anglé, et uo pa kontab. Koman ou vlépou-m ta rekomndé-ou pou travay sa-a-."* (Ti Tio, [one of my nicknames] your English and your driving skills are not too good, and you know nothing of accounting. How do you want me to recommend you for the job?)

I said, *"Pè Noël, anglé mouin bon é m'ka kondui. M'pa guin diplom mè mouin passé tout tan mouin ak Renel ché Laroche. M'ka di que mouin sé yon bookeeper. Mandé Renel si ou kouè ké mouin ap manti."* (Père Noël, my driving and English skills are good. Besides, I spent the whole time that Renel attended Chez Laroche learning accounting. I can say that I am a bookkeeper. If you think I am lying, you may ask Renel.)

At that point, Père Noël said, "Okay, I will recommend you, but please do not embarrass me." A brand new chapter of my life was about to begin. Père Noël called Mrs. Dalencour, Marie France, who referred the job to my brother Renel and told her that his second son, Joel, would be the one for the job, not Renel. Mrs. Dalencour asked him to send me for an interview. The guy who held the job previously had mysteriously disappeared. No one knew what had happened to him. Some said that he was killed, and others said he was arrested and put in jail under some-one else's name. I spent the night before the interview learning how to drive better and tried to practice my little English. We used my dad's car, which was a Peugeot 404 station wagon that could seat seven people comfortably. There were six in the car: Renel, Jarman, Fritz, Pierre-Richard, Carnold, and myself. Fritz was the master of everything. He was the sharpest and the most intelligent one. He would try to guess some of the questions the interviewer could ask and formulated the possible answers. It was a Thursday night. We had so much fun. We talked about the job, about how our life would be changed, and how much money to accept.

The interview was on Friday morning at 9:30 a.m. Père Noël had to go work, so we rented a car on that same day. The game began at 7:30 a.m. We did not sleep at all. We broke only to clean up and get dressed. Then we went to pick up the car rental. From there we went straight to the motor vehicles department, which we call in Haïti the *Department De La Circulation d'Haiti,* for the driver's license. At the bureau, I filled out the form and took the written test, which I passed with no sweat. The hard part was the road test. I got in the car with the officer, who asked me to start the car and told me where to go. Even before I took off, I told the officer that I needed the driver's license to get a job and that it was very important that I pass the test and obtain the driver's license. While I was talking with him, I pulled out a twenty-dollar bill and handed it to him. He told me to go up the street and come back in the bureau so he could get papers signed for the license.

Within twenty minutes, we were on our way to the company for the interview. I practiced my English one more time and when we arrived there, we prayed and moved toward the main entrance of the office. There I met with Mrs. Dalencour. I told her, *"Bonjour Madame, Je suis Joël Espérance, le fils de monsieur Noël Tingué. Je suis ici pour l'entrevue."* (Good morning Madam, I am Joel Esperance, the son of Mr. Noël Tingué. I am here for the interview.)

She answered, *"Bonjour Joel, Je suis Marie France Dalencour, attends un p'tit moment, je vais dire at Mr. Guidry que tu es ici."* (Good morning Joel, I am Marie France Dalencour. Hold on for a minute. I am going to tell Mr. Guidry that you are here.) Five to ten minutes later, I was introduced to my interviewer,

Mr. John Guidry, the assistant director of the project. Coincidently, he wore the same type of shirt that I wore the day of the interview. The only difference was his shirt was red and white and mine blue and white.

As I said earlier, I was about to face the real world. Mr. Guidry would not wear that shirt again, at least not to work. I worked for the company for one year and a half, and I did never see him wear it again to work. The gentleman asked me several questions, which I managed to answer the best I could. There were two questions that I had some difficulty answering. One was, "May I see your ID?" and the other one was, "How long you have been driving, and what kind of cars have you been driving?" First of all, I did not know what the term "ID" meant. If he had asked me for my identification card, I would have understood. Since he extended his hand toward me, I thought for a minute and told myself, *The man does not ask for money. So it has to be some types of papers.*

I reached into my coat pocket and handed him everything that I had in my pocket, which included my driver license, a letter of recommendation, and my identification card. He smiled and took the identification card. For the other question, I told him that I have been driving for four or five years, and I drove all kind of vehicles. I was offered the job with an unexpected salary, twice as much as what I thought they would give me to start. While I was being interviewed, the gang was outside waiting. You should have seen their faces when I announced the news to them. We went to the beach to celebrate. I was supposed to start the job on the following Monday.

The first week was great. I did not have to do too much because it was a period of orientation. On the second week, the fun began. I was asked to go downtown to run some errands. I was handed a car key and a few envelopes to drop at the post office and a few checks to cash at the bank. Well, I drove the car down the street a little way and parked it behind a gas station. I took a Tap Tap to go downtown to take care of my business. I did that for the entire week. On Friday, I received my first paycheck, a big one, and guess what! The gang was out there waiting for me. I cashed the check, and I shared it as follows: I took out the Tap Tap or taxi fees and divided the balance equally among my friends and myself. That practice did not continue, but I did help my friends monetarily from time to time and when there were some problems.

The challenge and the trouble grew a little more; the director of the company began to give me orders. He would personally ask me to take care of his private business. I was having some tough times understanding him. I would always try to interpret what he wanted. Sometimes I would get lucky and sometimes not. Unfortunately, I had a car accident on the third week of the job. I hit the president's Mom's private secretary's car. Technically I was wrong, but it was also the most frightening thing to happen to anyone. I could have been killed on the spot or gotten arrested. Thanks to the Almighty, I did not have any problem, but later on the police would intervene and find out where I was working. They decided to take the matter directly to my big boss, Mr. Ned Herring, who was not happy at all.

Two weeks later, Mr. Herring asked me to take him to the American Embassy and then to take him over to a friend's house up to the mountain. My inexperience and fear made it very awkward for me to drive the gentleman. Since I did not have a choice, I left with him, knowing that I was in for big trouble. Early in the trip, I began to go over the sidewalks and cut the wheel too much on curves. Mr. Herring did not like that. Along the way, he asked me to stay focused and to keep my head straight. We made it to the embassy. I said to myself, "One down, one to go." He came back and asked me to take him to the mountain, somewhere in Petionville. I was surprised; I made it up there with no sweat. On my way back, I was using one of the largest and smoothest roads, at that time, "La Route de Delmas." Maybe I was too confident. I was driving a little fast. Mr. Herring told me to slow down.

I did not understand what he said, as usual. I thought he asked me to go faster. I replied to him, "Yes sir." I went faster. He said, with a firm voice, "Slow down, Joel"

"Yes sir." I again replied. I went even faster. Then, he yelled, in a broken French, *"Monsieur, Je vous demnande d'arreter la voiture maintenant."* (Mister, I am asking you to stop the car immediately.) I was flabbergasted. I immediately stopped the car.

Then, with a strong conation, Mr. Herring said, "Sortez de la voiture." (Get out of the car.) I got out of the car. Then he said, *"Montez de l'autre côté"* Get in on the other side. I got in, and he slammed on the gas.

I said to myself, "The guy could have told me to go much faster. I would have done it." At that time, I did not know that when someone is upset he or she would have the urge to drive faster and roughly. Arriving back in the office, Mr. Herring went straight to Mrs. Dalencour and began to curse. I firmly believe that the guy called me all kinds of names. You know what I mean. I am Haitian and black. This is to help you to figure out what kind of names he probably called me. I could tell that he was extremely upset, but my lack of the English language at that time made it impossible to understand what he was saying.

A few minutes later, Marie France came toward me with the saddest face. I had never seen her that sad, and I would never see her that sad again. She said, "Joel, Mr. Herring m'a demandé de te révoquer. Il a dit que tu es un menteur, et que tu ne parles pas l'anglais, tu ne sais pas conduire, et que tu es un bluffeur." (Joel, Mr. Herring asked me to fire you. He said that you are a liar, you don't speak English, you don't know how to drive, and that you are a bluffer.) She asked me what happened. I explained to her that I thought I was doing well. I took him to the U.S. embassy and then to Petionville. On our way back, he said something to me. I assumed that he wanted me to go faster, so I did, but it seemed that was not what he meant. I asked her to ask him to give me a second chance, and I would prove to him that I was capable of doing them both. She said that she did not think he was going to give me a second chance. I told her that I really needed the job and that my family counted on me to help financially. She went into his office and asked him for me.

First, he refused. Then when Marie France pushed, he said, "I would do it with this condition: For thirty days Joel will never look me in the eyes. Every time he sees me, he will have to turn his head the other way. Also, I don't want him to sit at his desk, but in a corner, facing the wall."

Marie France came back with tears in her eyes and told me not to accept Mr. Herring's deal. I told her that I had to accept it for two reasons. First and the most importantly, if I left right then, the guy and everyone would remember me as a liar and a bluffer. I didn't want that to happen. Secondly, I really needed the money for my family and my friends. I cried like a baby that day. It was a sad and a horrible day. So, I made a vow to myself that I was going to improve my English and my driving within a thirty-day time period. I toughed it out, and I worked on it.

I always live by proverbs:

"Where there is the will there is the way."

"Some people dreamed dreams, while others woke up and worked hard at it."

"Happy are those who dream dreams and are ready to pay the price to make them come true."

Throughout the book, you will find that I lived by these proverbs. I practiced both the driving and the English tirelessly for a month. When the thirty days were up, Mr. Herring called me into his office and told me to get ready to take him to the American Embassy and then to Petionville. I said, "Whenever you are ready, sir."

He said, "Let's go now." We left the office. I could tell Marie France was so scared that she could not even wish me good luck. I could also tell that she thought that Mr. Herring would drop me somewhere downtown and come back by himself. I prayed and got in the car.

He got in and sat next to me and said, "Let's go." So we left. That day, I even impressed myself. I drove like a "pro." Then the moment for the real test came. "Joel, I would like for you to take me to Petionville."

"My pleasure, Mr. Herring," I replied. He looked at me and shook his head; we went up there and at the highest peak, I stopped the truck and I let go the brake while I maintained the truck on the same spot by using the clutch and the accelerator together for approximately five seconds, and I took off without a slide back. Mr. Herring asked me what that was about. I told him that I heard a noise and that I was trying to detect what it was.

He smiled and said, "That was not too bad."

Finally, we made it back beautifully, without any incident. We even had a few conversations on the roads. When we got back, he told Marie France that I was off the probation. Then he added that I was an intelligent man.

Now I was ready to undergo another test from Mr. Herring. Almost every morning, he would ask me to stop in the bank to get him some money. The way he did it was so obvious. He would write a check directly to me and ask me to cash it for him. After the third or fourth time, I realized that he never wrote the check for an even value. It always was for $177.00, $253.00, $359.00, $433.00, and I had a strange feeling when I caught him using an unusual behavior. He would not count the money when I gave it to him, and he would open the envelope that contained the cash without looking in it, grab a few dollars, and toss the envelope in a drawer in his desk. So, I began to develop a strategy as a counterattack. I would count the money three to four times before I gave it to him. He would write me a check for over $800.00 at a time to cash for him. That process continued for a month and a half.

One day, Mr. Herring's wife had a fight with her chauffer on her way home from a party. She was very drunk and not in a good mood. So the chauffer took her to the closest police station and dropped her there and quit. Mr. Herring had to go get her, because she could not drive herself home. The following day, Mr. Herring asked me to do him a favor and go get his wife at home and take her to a friend's house. I did him the favor. His wife was very happy and asked me to talk to her new chauffer about proper manners. On the following morning, Mr. Herring called me into his office and handed me an envelope with $150.00 and said to me, "My wife wants you to have this." I told him that I only did him a favor. He said, "Mrs. Herring would be very mad if you do not take the money." I took it.

In the following week, I was going to get an excellent reward, which sticks with me to this day. Mr. Herring called me into his office and he told me, "Joel, you are the most honest and intelligent man I have ever worked with. Everyone here in this office has a car but you. I want you to have a pickup truck that you will use every day. The truck is yours as long as the project is here in Haiti." He used to give me a gas coupon to fuel the car when needed. That day, he signed the whole coupons book and handed it to me. Then he added that famous sentence, "Joel, from today on, you are my son." That was the most glorious day of my life. I could not wait to go home to show off in my neighborhood.

When I got home, I explained what happened to me. Everyone was so happy that we had a party the same night. There I picked up a nickname: "P'tit Hosking." Automatically, I became a legend. I got more money on the job and a car. There was a group of great people working there who belonged to the upper class of the country. That means that I was mingling with the elites. I was invited to quite a few upscale parties. Pierre Richard, who was the controller for the project, invited me to go with him and a couple of other friends to Cap-Haitian, the second largest city in the country. It was an honor to be part of that group. Needless to say, I went with them. I had a friend, whom I will call TB, who was in medical school with my sister Edith. He came from the north part of the nation, Cap-Haitian. I asked him if he had anything that he would want to send to his parents. He asked me to say hello to his folks, and of course, he gave me their address. I was about to meet the prettiest girl in Cap-Haitian, Joliette, who later would be my girlfriend. I would break up with her because of an inferiority complex. I would have another chance a year or two later, but once again the romance would end hurtfully and mysteriously.

I went to TB's house, met with his parents, and chatted for a few minutes. Next thing I knew, a beautiful girl showed up. She politely said hello, and of course, embraced everyone. She had a pretty and adorable smile. There was another sister, an older one in the house. We asked their dad, who was chief physician and/or director in one of the major hospitals in the city, if we could take his daughters to a party in one of the most prestigious nightclubs in the city. Since I was introduced as one of TB's best friends, we were not turned down. That night, while dancing with Joliette, I took a look at her, and she smiled. Her teeth were white and brilliant. I saw the brightest, most beautiful smile that I ever saw in my life. She kept smiling, and the beauty of it was the night-club had some black lights so her teeth were florescent under the light. I said to myself, "She will be mine; it will just be a matter of time."

We had, or at least I had, a fantastic time in Cap-Haitian. That was her last year in secondary school. She was to come to Port-au-Prince for her final national test. We became good friends and started to go out. It was somewhat funny, because we both had somewhat similar names. She called me P'tit Jo, and I called her Jolie. Meanwhile, she was admitted to the medical school, and as I stated earlier, I could not get into the law school. I was not too happy about having a *Med Student* as a girlfriend while I was a *Messenger*. I could always picture, in my mind, her coming up the street where I lived to see me almost every afternoon. Her mom was not too happy with the fact that her brother used to go out with one of my sisters, so I did not treat her bad. That was not a concern of mine. I loved her very much. I just, for the first and the last time of my life, felt inferior. And I blew it.

There was a very young and beautiful girl in the neighborhood whose name was Bebita. She was probably the most arrogant girl in the area. I don't know if arrogant is the word to describe her. Maybe overconfident is a better term. Yes, we had dated each other. We had a great time, and I am not proud to say that she was the only girl that I let control me at that time. It could have been because she was the youngest. With all those girls, I thought that I was "the King of the Block." I was at my prime time. I want to clear something up. I never treated any of my girlfriends badly. Besides, all of them were highly respected and from dignified parents. I have an absolute respect for them all to this date. I remain good friend with most of them. And they were all well educated socially and academically. We share mutual respect, and somehow, our love was pure in many ways and shapes. That is why I said, I remain good friend with most of them, those that I have the chance of meeting again.

Most people know this proverb: *Après le beau temps, c'est la pluie.* (After the good time, it is bad time.) My life was about to take a wrong turn, which would almost be fatal. It was early in the month of August 1977. Honorable Ambassador Andrew Young was coming to Haiti, and I was supposed to pick him up at the airport. I was looking forward to that day, even though I did not know what kind of person he was at that time. Now, you remember that I mentioned previously that the gentleman who had my job before had mysteriously disappeared. But for the grace of God, I would not have disappeared, I would have been dead.

A few days before the arrival of Ambassador Young in Haiti, I went to work as happy as I had ever been. As usual, I got my assignments, which most of the time included a trip to downtown. I got there at or around 10:30 a.m. I decided after I ran my errands to stop at my usual snack bar for a hamburger. I asked for the hamburger and a glass of orange juice. I took a few bites of the hamburger and found that it had a bad taste. I automatically stopped eating it, and I drank the orange juice. Suddenly, I felt very uncomfortable, but I went back to the office. I later on ended up leaving early. On my way home, I felt worse. I had a severe stomachache. At home, I went straight to bed, but the pain was getting worse. At about 7:30 p.m., I told my brother Renel it was best that we go to the hospital. So we went. There I was treated and released. The diagnosis was food poisoning. We went back home. I took the medicine that was prescribed to me, and I fell asleep. I woke up with worst abdominal pain. I went outside and started throwing up. I threw up a green, extremely sour liquid. I was very scared. I said to myself, "Fiel moin pété." (My liver blew up) I jumped in the house, woke up Renel, and told him that I was dying and that we had to go back to the hospital immediately.

One to two hours after arriving at the hospital, I got admitted, and at 6:30 a.m., I began to pass blood from my bowels. I was scared to death. I started to cry. I thought that I was going to die, and I felt that my life was just beginning. I had a job, a few of my brothers and my mom were in the U.S., and I knew that it was a matter of time before I could go to the U.S. I was given a truck to drive to work and about. I had a few girlfriends. And I really wanted to live.

Then I also began to think about the previous chauffeur's disappearance. I said to myself, *Joel, kom yo pa ka fè-ou disparèt, yo empoisonin ou.* (Joel, since they could not make you disappear, they poisoned you.) Early in the morning, the doctors began to work on me. Lab tests revealed that I had a serious intestinal infection. One of the doctors suggested that my family contact a surgeon immediately. They did so. The surgeon ordered more testing be done and told my family that he would like to see if there would be some improvement. The matter got worse. I began to experience an excruciating abdominal pain, but the doctor did not yet want to perform the operation. I was left like that for the whole day, taking "antispasmodic" and other pain medicine and some penicillin. On the second day in the hospital, the doctor conducted a final test that revealed I had a more severe infection and, according to the doctor, I had only a fifteen percent chance to survive. Then he agreed to perform the surgery under two conditions: one, he wanted $5,000.0 0 up front and $2,000.00 later, and two, to move me in a private hospital. Knowing the percentage chance of survival, I declined to be operated on by that doctor.

Since my sister Edith was an intern and my sister Guilaine was a nurse, the chief surgical resident, Dr. Duvernacle Duclerville, decided to perform the surgery. The surgery was scheduled for 3:30 p.m. the following day. The schedule was conditional. If the pain stopped, the doctor would not go ahead with it. And if the pain continued or amplified, he would proceed as planned. Something strange happened in the morning that the surgery was scheduled. I woke up with no pain, no discomfort, nor did I feel sick. I automatically knew that I was in trouble, and for a while, I even thought that I was dead. There was no way that anyone would have the kind of pain that I had one day before and then wake up feeling so pain-free. Dr. Duclerville came to see me during his hospital visits. He told me that if I continued to feel that way, he would not operate on me. My family was relieved to the fact that I felt better and that I was not going to die. I called Renel and said to him, *"Fréro, pou jan m'tap souffri tout semaine nan, li impossible pou souffrans moin ta fini konsa."* (Brother, for the amount of pain that I had been having in the past week, it would have been impossible for the pain to stop just like that.) Around 3:00 p.m., the doctor stopped by to check on me. I was still pain-free. He told me that he was on standby and had the room available in case the pain came back.

Since I was feeling so good, most of my friends came to visit. Among them there were a few of my girlfriends in the room at the same time, Jessiline, Nanty, Danienne, Bebita, Malie, and Joliette. I was not in a regular room like most hospitals. I was in a hall that was more like a field army hospital. The hall was divided in two, one side for males and the other side for females. All patients were under one roof. In my area, there were about fifty patients arranged with twenty-five on each side. We were all patients either awaiting surgery or recovering from surgery. While I was surrounded by girlfriends and family, one of the girls, I don't remember who, was using a piece of cardboard to fan me. She was fanning me for a long period of time. After one hour or so, Bebita said to her, *"Passem paravent an, dailleur ou pa gain ou bras électric."* (Pass me the fan; besides you don't have an electrical arm.) After twenty years or so, I would see Bebita again. She still remembered her action. Around 7:00 p.m., most of visitors had gone. There were three visitors left: Renel, his girlfriend at that time, Chantal, and Jessiline. Renel married Chantal four years later. They are still married as I write this book.

I called Renel and asked him to get closer so I could tell him something. I told him that as soon as he took the ladies home, I would start screaming to alert the doctors. He asked why I wanted to do something like that, especially when I was no longer in pain. I reassured him that it was impossible for me to not be in pain. I asked him to come right back. So, they left. As I said, I began to cry out loud. I screamed with pain, and I asked the attending nurse to call the doctor. Dr. Duclerville came right away. He asked me what was going on. I told him that I was in such pain that I could not breathe. He said, "I am going to operate on you right away."

He asked the nurse and the doctors to get ready. I felt like I was delivered from fire. After a few minutes, Renel came back and called my parents to come down for the surgery. A little bit after 9:00 p.m. I was lying on the operating table. The surgery began around 9:30 p.m. and lasted seven and a half hours.

True enough, Dr. Duclerville said, "If you had not had the surgery that night, you would have died the following day." What would have happened? I would have developed a peritonitis infection. Anyway, I was diagnosed with "Intestinal Necrosis and Perforated Appendicitis," *Nécrose Intestinale, et Perforation d'Appendicite.* I don't want to say that I was lucky, because that would be wrong. I want to say that I was blessed. There is no way that I could have survived that ordeal if God did not have a purpose for me. I saw many signs of His grace and blessing along the way. Thus far, I can say as it says in the Book of Philippians 3:13–14: "Brothers, I have not yet arrived, but I forgot what I went through and I am striving for what lies ahead." I will quote this verse in other chapters as I move along.

When I regained conscience, I thought I was still on the operating table. I asked my brother Renel if he could ask someone to put me on a bed. He told me that I was already on a bed.

I asked him why my body was so sore. It would be a while before I would realize what happened to me. I was told that during the surgery, all my intestines were removed from my body and put outside so they could operate on them. So all that time, I was on my back. And the worst was the operating table did not have a pad on it. That was why I was so uncomfortable. I spent thirteen days in the hospital. During that time, I saw two young men die right in front of my eyes. That was an experience that I was going to re-live again after twenty-seven years. Yes, I witnessed an old friend of mine die right before my eyes while I was visiting him in a hospital. My friend was only forty-seven years old.

While I was in the hospital, I was not supposed to eat for the first seven days. I would smell the food every day, in the morning, noon, and the evening. Can you imagine how I felt for the seven days that I had to spend without eating rice? I began to eat very little on the eighth day after the surgery. Gradually, I ate a little bit more and more. I had one thing on my mind—eat a large plate of white rice with pureed green peas and meatballs. After I spent thirteen days in the hospital, I got discharged. I went home and asked my aunt to cook that special meal for me. And besides, the day following my release was a Sunday. Sundays were, and probably still are, the day that most Haitians would eat large and expensive meals. She was so happy to cook the meal as a way of celebrating my release and to honor the tradition. Since everyone had thought that I was going to die, it was not that big of a deal to prepare a meal at my request. There were so many people who came to visit me that day. I was so weak that I could barely talk. I spent most of the time smiling and listening to my guests.

When the meal was ready, I ate the food with "a fury," which means I overate. I was about to take a turn for the worse. After I finished eating, I lay down for a while, and I fell asleep. I woke up in the evening with a minor abdominal pain, but I made nothing of it. I went back to sleep with no sweat. It had been a long day; I was happy as the night was approaching. I was about to spend a night in my own bed. Remember that the bed was a twin bed that my brother Renel and I shared, but after the surgery, I was to sleep in it by myself.

I woke up the following day in a different world; that was the first night that I had spent for a long time without listening to people crying, screaming with pain. The next morning, things were normal and the day was developing quite well. In the middle of the day, I began to experience a more severe pain than the one that I felt the day before. The pain was increasing from moderate to excruciating. I was about to develop an "intestinal occlusion." It was so obvious that anyone could see the separation between my stomach and my abdomen. I was passing out.

I was so scared and so much in pain that my entire family was in tears. At that point, I said to myself, *C'est fini, Je vais mourir pour de bon.* (It's over; I am dying for good). Two days out of the hospital, I was on my way back. When I arrived at the hospital, the doctor said that I was too weak to undergo another operation, and besides, it would have been too risky to reopen me. At that time, I was in and out of consciousness. They were to make a quick and accurate decision. Since surgery was out of the question, there was only one thing to do—administer a *Lavement* fleet enema. The risk was if the threads loosened during the process, the liquid would penetrate through the cut and go directly in the "péritonite." If that happened, I would develop "peritonitis," and I would die. If that did not happen, the liquid would unplug the intestine, and the "aliment" that was in the stomach would flow and I would be fine, at least for a while.

Now, they needed someone to sign an authorization form permitting the doctor to perform the procedure. That was the saddest day of the Esperance and the Tingue family that I know of. My sister Edith signed the paper. They had someone pray for me and the family, and they began the procedure. Everyone was so scared, even the doctors. The process seemed to take an eternity. In reality, it did not take any more than ten minutes. First, I felt a tremendous pressure and suddenly, I felt like someone was lifting me, and I immediately lost control of my body. I said, *"Merci Jésus, Je suis sauvé."* (Thank you Jesus, I am delivered.) When I regained consciousness, some of my family members were sitting on the floor next to my bed, and the rest were standing around the bed.

That time I spent seventeen days in the hospital. The doctors did not want to take any chances by letting me go home without making sure that I was okay. To my big surprise, Mr. Herring came to see me in the hospital. He asked my family to move me to a private hospital on his account, but my doctors would not have been able to care for me there. So we thanked him very much, but I stayed in the public hospital. The pickup truck stayed in front of my house for more than four weeks. Mr. Herring had thought that I was going to go back to work soon. He sent someone to come to get it while I was in the hospital the second time. I left the hospital that time with a new attitude. I would not be eating for a while, not because I was told not to, but because I was afraid. I stayed over at my sister Ruth's house to avoid talking too much. There, Mrs. Dalencour and Mrs. Herring came to visit and brought some fruit and money for me. Mr. Herring came back to visit and asked me if I wanted to borrow some money from the company. I graciously told him that I did not want to borrow any money. I really did not need the money at that time, but when he asked me to borrow the money, he knew that the company's contract was about to end. If I had borrowed the money, I would not have been required to give it back. As of today, I think that I did the right thing. After I got released by my doctor to go back to work, I found out that the company was about to close. I went back to work anyway and spent only three to four months working. Mr. Herring later helped me to find a job at the United States Agency for International Development (USAID) as a driver.

TWENTY-THREE YEARS OLD TO TWENTY-FIVE YEARS OLD

Working for the US Government

I began to work in the motor pool area as a driver. This job was different from when I worked for Western Sonderegger. There were many drivers available to drive diplomats and run errands. We all reported to a dispatcher who ran the motor pool. Upon receiving a call, the dispatcher would deploy a chauffeur with a car that suited the needs of the person who requested the ride. Our duties were to pick up the person from the office or home, to drive that person around wherever he or she needed to go, and/or take him or her home or to the office. Sometimes, we would deliver and pick up some appliances or do other errands as needed.

There again, at the USAID, I had to face some humiliations. Some of the diplomats were very personable, while others were not. One particular man, whom I call Mr. Jones, called one day and asked for a car and a chauffeur. I was assigned to take him to his destination. No one in the group liked him. He always found ways to humiliate us. To my recollection, he was the only diplomat that would sit in the backseat while being driven around. I had no choice but to pick him up at the office to take him to the Faculty of the Agronomy of Port-au-Prince. Mr. Jones got in the car and sat in the backseat and to the right. I drove him there and waited outside for a good four hours, sitting under a mango tree chatting with some merchants. Right in front of them, Mr. Jones came out with a friend and ordered me to open the back doors so they could get in. Let me tell you this. Neither one had any more then a light briefcase in hands. It was purely to humiliate me that he asked me to open the doors. I wasn't going to do it, but I remembered the quote from the French author, *"Nul ne se connait, tant qu' il n' a pas souffert."* (No one knows what he is made of until he is tested.) I came to realize that it was just another bridge to cross. I brushed it off and opened the door for both of them and drove them back to the office.

On the way back, I faced a greater obstacle than driving the two men. I came across one of my girlfriends who was going somewhere. I could not afford to let her see me behind a wheel driving the two gentlemen around. In Haiti, it is a question of class and prestige, not race and color. People actually lie to cover their identities because a person is judged on what he appears to be, not who he really is. The kind of ladies that I used to go out with would not give me any attention if they found out that I was a chauffeur. It was good to be working, but I had to lie about what I was doing for a living. Now you can imagine how I felt when I spotted the girl. I kept my head straight and inflated my mouth like a balloon in a way to disguise myself so she could not identify me. Luckily, she did not. I almost had a heart attack that day.

Meanwhile, there was a young gentleman, I call him Mario, who was working in the organization as a (GSA,) General Services Assistant. His job primarily was to assist the diplomats and VIPs arriving in Haiti by picking them up at the airport, putting them in a furnished apartment, and arranging their accommodations during their stay. The fellow was so fortunate, that when his parents picked him up at the airport, they presented him with a gift, a brand new BMW, to welcome him back to Haiti. He landed one of the best jobs in the organization, which would be mine in the next few months. Anyway, a couple months later, to my big surprise, I was informed by the General Services Officer (GSO) that Mario did not want to stay in the organization and that he planned to resign very soon. The GSO wanted me to apply for the position. So I did and fortunately I got it. On my last working day in the motor pool, I was asked to pick up Mr. Jones from his office to take him to the Agriculture Department. I didn't make anything of it. I went to his office, picked him and a friend up, and I took them to their destination. As usual, he asked me to wait in the yard for them. It was about 9:00 a.m. when we got there, and when they came back at 2:00 p.m., I was still sitting there waiting for them. I had to make a tough decision. I could leave them there or call the dispatcher to send another chauffeur to pick them up. Since I wanted to teach Mr. Jones a lesson, I left them there without telling them or calling for a backup chauffeur. Of course, I did wrong. If I have to do it again, I would wait for as long as it would take and take them back. *Two wrongs do not make it right.* My rationalization was, I had already received the promotion in writing. Therefore, there was nothing they could have done to me. Wow!

Nevertheless, Mr. Jones was very upset. Apparently, they came out and saw no one there. I understand they waited for a great while for someone to pick them up. Mr. Jones brought a complaint against me. Like I said, it was too late to do anything about it. In my new position, I was treated like a prince. I loved what I was doing, and I got full respect from other members of the organization and my new peers. I got the greatest kicks out of the position. One aspect of the job was to go to the airport to pick up VIPs. I had an American Diplomat Pass in my pocket. I didn't have any problem getting inside of the airport. I had full clearance everywhere I went. I was at my prime. No one will ever understand the amount of privileges I had if they aren't Haitian. Meanwhile, my mom had already applied for a permanent visa for us to live in the U.S.A. I wanted to visit the country before I resided there. Since I was an employee of the USAID, I did not have any problem in obtaining a tourist visa to visit the U.S.A.

In Haiti at that time, going to the U.S.A. for vacation was super. I left Haiti to spend a couple weeks there. I felt so good. All my friends went to the airport to say goodbye to "papa." It was like a president of a country leaving for foreign soil. I boarded the plane for the first time in my life bound for the U.S.A. My final destination was New York. While I was there, my family took me to many places of great attraction and sightseeing. I couldn't wait to go back home so I could show off. As a way of clarification, my leaving Haiti to visit the U.S. was not that impressive for the well-to-do people. The rich people were on a constant *va et vient* mode from abroad. I am not going to lie to you. It was a heck of a deal for my entourage and me. Even though it was always a big deal when anyone came back from vacationing in the U.S., I made an exceptionally triumphant return to Haiti. Right after I came back, I bought my first car, a 1974 Honda Civic. The car was not in good shape, but it was a car that served its purposes. I was about to enter into the next best phase in my entire life.

Brand New Chapter of My Life

After my older adopted sister, Edith, graduated from medical school, she got married to Elie Celestin who was her medical study and residency partner. On June 21, 1978, they had their first child, the beautiful Sarah Jane, who is now a practicing physician as well. I was honored to be chosen as Sarah's godfather. That action was going to change my life forever. On the christening day, I dressed to kill. I wore a light green suit (bellbottoms) and a white tuxedo style shirt with a white and green bowtie. The shoes that I wore matched my complete outerwear. I looked so good that I fell in love with my own self. I drove my beat up Honda to the church.

For some reason, I did not enter the church immediately. I stayed outside for a few minutes observing some activities. Of course, I saw a few girls that I knew and some with whom I was good friends. I went to chat with them. One of the girls was teasing me, by calling me *Le Parrain* (Godfather). Suddenly, I spotted a beautiful girl out there. To my big surprise, she walked straight toward me and said, *"Bonjour Parrain"* (good morning godfather), and she kissed me on the cheek.

I said, *"Bonjour mademoiselle"* (good morning Miss). Then I left the area and went inside the church. The young girl was well dressed. She had the brightest smile a person could have had. I asked my adopted sister Guilaine, who was the godmother of Sarah, if she knew the girl or if the girl was a nurse. I asked that question because I had spent a lot time in the hospital when I was so sick, and I met quite a few nurses that were very good to me. My sister at that time was a nurse. So, more than likely, she would have recognize her if she were a nurse. I insisted that she ask her anyway. The girl told my sister that she was not a nurse. I fell in love with her on the spot. I tried to get her name, but it was not possible. I left the church that day saying to myself, *In the event that I see her again, I will court her and I will marry her.*

The following Sunday, I went back to the same church expecting to see her. Yes, indeed I saw her, but I could not talk to her because an old friend of mine, Maude, would not let me talk to the mysterious girl. After three consecutive Sundays of trying, I gave up. Three months later, on a weekday, I saw the mysterious girl again, except that time she was on her way to a daytime movie with a well known *Karatéka* (Karaté man) in Haïti, whom I will call "P'tit Pierre." They were walking handin-hand toward a movie theater. I was on my way back to the office when I spotted them. I was in a brand new Suburban that was white and blue, had bulletproof windows, and a license plate that said "Corps Diplomat." I said to the chauffeur, *"Fais tourner la voiture immédiatement, Je viens juste de revoir ma future femme."* (Make a U-turn immediately. I just saw my future wife.) The gentleman immediately made a U-turn and moved toward them. He slowed down as we were approaching them. I gently waved at her and surprisingly, she waved back with a smile that said, "I remember you." Then I waved goodbye. She did the same. Unfortunately, I could not ask for any information. Three more months had elapsed, and still I did not have any luck.

One bright morning, I had to go to work. I believe it was a Saturday. I found out that I had a flat tire. So I left the car at home and decided to take a taxi. Remember, I lived in a dead end area. In order to catch a cab, I had to walk down the street to the main road and walk to a four-way street corner a few feet away from where my street joined the main road.

While waiting for a cab, I stood up on the other side of the street facing a bakery named "God Is Good," located in the corner of *Rue Monseigneur Gilloux et Route des Dalles*. The bakery belonged to a fairly rich businessman named Belony Salomon. Mr. Salomon was a well-known gentleman in the neighborhood. Most people called him "Bello." While I was standing there, a young man approached and said to me, *"Ti madmoizel qui sou caise la, ap rélé-ou."* (The bakery's cashier, a young lady, would like to see you.) I told him to tell her I was Joel Esperance and to ask if she was sure that I was the one she wanted to talk to. He went and talked to the lady and came back. He told me that the lady said she did not know what my name was, but I was the one she wanted to talk to. Unwillingly, I proceeded toward the bakery, and as I was entering the door, I could not believe my eyes. The mysterious girl was sitting behind the cash register. I said to myself, "The first time in my life I decide to marry a woman, she happens to be a cashier." I continued to walk toward her; I could not stop. I began to wonder what in the world I was going to say to her. She was indeed very pretty with the brightest smile on her face. The last time I saw a gorgeous smile like that was at *Feu Vert,* which was one of the most prestigious nightclubs in Cap-Haitian at that time. That was when I met Joliette for first time.

I also smiled and said, *"Bonjour mademoiselle, vous travaillez ici?"* (Good morning Miss. Are you working here?)

She answered, *"Bonjour Monsieur, non, Je ne travaille pas ici. Je suis venue voir mon père et je me suis décidée à l'aider avec la caisse."* (Hello Monsieur. No, I am not working here. I came to see my dad, and I decided to help with the cash register.)

I said to myself, *She is lying, b*ecause *most youngsters would tell you they were related to Bello, since Bello was one of the richest men and well known in the area.* That was why I thought she was lying. I smiled. I continued to talk to myself. I said, *The very first time I meet a lady, I said that I would marry her in the event that I meet her again.* (I was thinking that I would have gone through the normal process: courtship, engagement, and marriage.) *Here we meet again, but there is no way that I am going to marry a cashier. I don't think so.*

Then I told her that I did not know that Mr. Salomon had a girl. She would not stop smiling. Then, she said, "Of course, he has a girl. I don't live here. I live with my grandparents."

Still, I did not believe her. Then I said, "By the way, I am Joel. Joel Esperance. What is your name?"

She said, "I am Marie Kettline. Marie Kettline Salomon."

I asked her how long she was planning to stay at her dad's house. She said for the whole day and that she would be going to her grandparents' in the evening. I asked her if it was okay for me to come back to see her around noon. She said yes, providing that I didn't come inside of her house and that I didn't ask for her. I was starting to believe her. We set up a time for me to be around her house. Then I left.

I asked the first person I met that I thought knew Mr. Salomon if Mr. Salomon had other children besides Wickny. Most people knew Mr. Salomon's son, because he was always in the house or driving his dad's cars around. The gentleman that I asked told me that Mr. Salomon had two other children besides Wickny. They were Kettline and Gladimir.

I found a taxi in front of her dad's bakery to take me to my workplace. In the office, I asked the dispatcher to give me the best car we had in the motor pool for a trip to Petionville. He did not ask why. Usually when you request a vehicle, you must have a chauffeur. So I asked for a friend of mine to be chauffeur, the same friend who happened to be with me three months earlier when I had spotted Kettline with the karaté man on their way to the movie. Both requests were approved. I told my friend that I had met that mysterious girl, and I knew where she lived. I explained to him that had I told the dispatcher we were to going to Petionville, but in reality we weren't. Instead, we were going to see the mysterious girl. Kettline asked the same kid who came to tell me that she wanted to see me to watch for me and to get her when I arrived. The minute the kid saw me, he went in to get Kettline. She came out immediately and started to smile the same way she had before. She told me that she didn't think I was going to come back. I chatted with her for few minutes under tight security. I asked her if it was okay if I stopped by to see her at her grandparents' house that evening. She told me it was okay but only in front of the house, not to come inside. I asked her why. She said her parents would not be happy with her if she allowed me in the house.

I said, "I understand. I would feel the same way, but I am going to stop by just to see you. You will need to stay outside in front of the house." I told her that I would be driving a gray Honda Civic. I could not wait to tell the world that I saw the mysterious lady and that she was no longer a mystery. I told my folks the news. Everyone was so happy for me, but none of them thought that I was really going to go out with her steadily. That was when I realized the way they perceived me was going to be a problem. Anyway, I was pumped, and I did not want to mess up my first date with her. I cleaned the car inside and out.

Let me remind you about some of the Honda's details. It was a 1974 Honda Civic. It was not very impressive and was in need of some repairs. We were in 1978, which means the car was only four years old. Those four years were equivalent to twelve years in comparison to car treatment in the U.S. The roads in Haiti are very bad and rocky. I describe it as a "beat up" car, but at that time, not everyone could own even a "beat up" car. So I was one in a few that could, which automatically made me a "little Bourgeois." I got in my car and went down to see Kettline. It was a February afternoon around 6:00 p.m.; the sun was still up and people were everywhere.

As I approached her house, I saw her standing with her relatives and friends, minus her grandparents that she called Mom and Dad. She lived off the main street, which was the busiest and most commercial street in Port-au-Prince. There were all kinds of businesses around; high-rise hotels, restaurants, and snack bars, to name a few. As a matter of fact, her grandparents had a small snack bar in front of their house. I wanted to impress her. So I decided to drive past the house and go down the street, making a sharp U-turn, I spun my wheels, and came to a stop in front of her house. She thought I had missed the house, and she started to run after the car to alert me. At the time, I increased the speed so I could hold the brakes while making the U-turn in a sliding mode. It may sound stupid, but at that time it was cool. So, she stopped and went back thinking, "He missed the house, and maybe I won't see him this evening." It did not take me any more than a few seconds to do my thing. I got out of the car and said hello to everyone. She introduced me to her great aunt, Mrs. Seïde, and then to the other folks. I felt like I had won a million dollars. I chatted with them for a minute. Then I offered to buy everyone ice cream, which they accepted.

I knew that she was the one I wanted to marry. I told her a little bit about my family and my background. Because I wanted to move fast, I did not waste any time. I asked her that same night if she had a boyfriend. She told me that she did have a boyfriend but not a steady one and she didn't know if she was even still going out with the guy.

I am in! Big time! I always had and still have the greatest confidence in myself. That's why I knew it was not going to be a problem, even if she was going steady with the other guy. We talked a little bit, and I left with the promise that I was coming to see her the next day. After a few "street visits," I told her that I was not going to stand outside of her house anymore and that I was going to go inside. She begged me not to do that unless I did not want to see her anymore. I explained to her that it was not good for her to have a young man standing in front of her house talking to her on a regular basis. I gave her a few reasons why it was not doing us any good. Knowing that I was going to marry her, I did not want people to form bad opinions or to have bad impressions about her. We debated on the issue for a week. On the following week, I went to see her, and I bluntly told her that I was going to go inside and welcome myself into the living room.

She thought that I was kidding, but I went straight in. I met with her grandmother. I said, "Bonsoir Madame Salomon." (Good evening, Mrs. Salomon.)

She answered, "Bonsoir Monsieur." (Good evening, Monsieur.)

I continued, "Je suis Joel Fils Espérance, l'enfant du pasteur Joël Espérance et un ami de Wickny. Est ce qu' il est la ou est ce que Je peux parler a Kettline?" (I am Joel Esperance Junior, Pastor Joel Esperance's son, and I am a friend of Wickny. Is he home? Or may I speak to Kettline please?)

She said, "Wickny n'est pas la, mais Kettline y est. Je vais l'appeller pour vous. Et quel est le nom de votre père encore?" (Wickny is not here, but Kettline is. And what is your dad's name again?)

I said, "Pastor Joël Espérance."

She said, "Je crois avoir rencontré votre père." (I think I have met your dad.) Then, she asked me to come in and wait for Kettline.

Why did I introduce myself to her like that? I knew that they were Christians, and that Wickny was very involved in church activities. My dad was not a well-known minister in Haïti, so Grandma did not know him. That was the way I made my entrée in the family. I quickly utilized my Christian background and my personal approach skills to integrate into the family. I became good friends with Mr. Salomon, Sr. I actually spent more time talking with them than with Kettline. Meanwhile, Kettline and I agreed to go out secretly. I never wanted to do anything stupid that could hurt our relationship and/or her relationship with her parents. One day her father, Mr. Salomon, Jr., was going to take the family out as a way to welcome home one of their relatives who had come to visit from the U.S.A. Kettline wanted me to go also. At that time, we were not officially dating, so I asked her to find out where they were going, and I would be there. Going there was not the problem, but rather how I was going to dance with her or talk to her. I found out that they were going to a disco restaurant called "Le Lamby Nightclub Restaurant" for dinner and dancing. I went there also, taking one of my biological sisters, Marie France, with me. I let Kettline know where we were and every time they played a song, I would go onto the floor with my sister, and Kettline took a cousin of hers that she trusted on the floor. Then we would switch partners with each other. So I would dance with Kettline and her cousin with my sister. It was a beautiful evening. Kettline and I were so happy, and we had a marvelous time.

After that evening, I decided to tell Mr. Salomon, Sr., about my relationship with Kettline. It was not a big deal because they trusted me so much. I told him about the relationship. He told me that he felt that there was something between Kettline and me. He warned me about his son's character. Mr. Salomon, Jr., was very, and I mean very, overprotective of her.

I took Grandpa for a trip up to the mountains. We went to Jacmel, the fourth city of the country, located in the southeast. Kettline and my sister Ruth went with us. We spent the whole day at the beach, toured the city in the evening, and went back home. Kettline and I had our first kiss there. I also discovered that Grandpa truly loved me. During that trip, we developed a close relationship.

Talking about a great relationship, I remember one day Kettline and I had a fight. That day, I decided I was not going to see her in the evening. I said a while ago that when I went there I usually spent most of my time with Grandpa, if not all of it. So that evening, Grandpa waited for me beyond my normal hour. I did not show up. In the morning, he asked Kettline what happened to me and why I did not come. Kettline, who did not want to tell him that we had a fight, decided to lie and told him that I was sick. He asked Kettline if she knew where I lived. She did not want to let him know that she knew where I lived because it would have made her look bad. But she knew very well where I lived. She told him that I lived somewhere around the Sainte Caridade Church, which was about four miles from their house. That was not a total lie, because I really did live around that area, but she could have told him on what street.

I did not go to their house at all that evening. So, the poor guy got up in the morning and walked to the area around the church asking everyone he met if they knew who Joel was and where exactly he lived. After a few hours without any success he went back home. He called Kettline aside and told her about his hard day looking for my house. She felt bad and sent someone to tell me about the situation and asked me to come to her house. I did. Grandpa was so happy to see me. He made sure that he gave me a sweater to wear so I would not get sick again. That particular evening, I asked him if I could marry Kettline. He said it would be fine with him, but his son would not be happy about it. We began to develop a strategy on how we would break the news to Kettline's father. I loved her so much. I always wanted to have a girl that I would consider to be a friend, a wife, and a mom at the same time. Kettline was all those things to me. I felt so good when I was near her. We went out clandestinely.

We drove around without having a place to go. We enjoyed each other very much. I told her about the first time I saw her, when I said that I would marry her if I had the chance to go out with her. She asked me if I was going to keep my promise. I said, "Yes, with all my heart."

Meanwhile, my brother Renel and I bought a new automobile, a white Fiat 727. At that time, my life took a new turn. My life in Haiti was great; I had a good job, a nice car, a beautiful girlfriend, and was a couple hundred dollars a week away from being broke. From Miragoâne to Port-au-Prince, I was on my way to the U.S. for good. As I stated before, there were a number of folks who lived in the U.S.A. as immigrants. They filed petitions on behalf of their kids who still remained abroad. My mom had applied for permanent American visas for my sister Marie France and me, and the visas were granted with no sweat. I did not want to leave the country then because I had so much "business" to take care of. Besides, I did not want to leave Kettline yet. I decided to stay in Haiti for another three months. Meanwhile, I was facing a great challenge in meeting Kettline's biological dad. Grandpa told me that he and I would have to go to face his son, because if he found out that Grandpa let me get in the house without letting him know what was going on, Mr. Salomon Jr. would be extremely upset, and he would not forgive Grandpa. I set up an appointment with Grandpa to go. The suit that I wanted to wear for that day got stolen. I thought that was bad luck, but I wore something else. I picked up Grandpa, and we went to Mr. Salomon Jr.'s house up the hill. Grandpa promised that he was going all the way with me. I have to say that Grandpa was taking a big chance. Of course, Grandpa confirmed the appointment with his son on my behalf. We arrived there at about 7:00 p.m. and were welcomed by Mrs. Salomon. We entered their living room and sat down. Mr. Salomon Jr. lay on a couch wearing a white short pants and a white Polo T-shirt. He did not sit properly on the couch, and he did not look at me directly.

Anyway, I decided to make my plea. I told Mr. Salomon that I loved his daughter and that I would like to marry her one day. Note that I said, "one day." The guy did not look at me while I was talking. He took a deep breath, and he said, "Quel est votre âge?" (How old are you?)

"Vingt cinq." (Twenty five.)

Then he sat down and took a straight look at me, and he said, "Est ce que vous savez quel âge a Kettline? (Do you know how old Kettline is?)

I said, "Non." (No)

He shook his head, and said, "Elle vient d' avoir dix- sept ans." (She just turned seventeen.) I explained to him that I was not going to have a normal girlfriend/boyfriend relationship with Kettline, and I could have seen her outside of her house and around her school, but instead I decided to come see her father. He told me that he appreciated my behavior, but he advised me to come back when she was ready. I asked him if I could visit her once and a while. I meant to say put her on "Layaway" for me.

"Negative," he answered.

Grandpa stood up and asked to talk to his son in my defense. Mr. Salomon Jr. listened carefully to his father. Then he took a good minute of silence, after which he asked me to bring my parents over to his house so he could talk with them. I told him that my parents were in the U.S., and that I was living in my godfather's household, and two of my biological sisters were here in Haiti. He said that it was okay to come with my godfather and one of my sisters. At that time, I knew that I was in. I asked Grandpa if he were ready to go so I could take him home. Mr. Salomon Jr. told me that I could leave, and then he would take his dad home. I did not think anything of it, because I really wanted to go home myself so I could talk to Père Noël.

To my big surprise, Père Noël turned me down. His reasons were: He did not want to be embarrassed. He thought I was going to deceive him. I had too many girlfriends, and he was afraid he might get arrested. I gave him my word. That was not enough. So I threatened him. I told him that I would leave the country the next day because I just found out that I was not as loved as I thought. And then he would never see me again. I knew that was going to bother him. He gave up and agreed to go with me. I went through the same thing with my sister. It was even worse trying to persuade her. Finally, I told my sister if she would not go there with me, I would ask her to go for a ride with me to the highest point in the country on an excursion. Then at the top of the mountain, I would roll the car down the hill with both of us in it. I won that battle also.

A couple of days later, I called Mr. Salomon Sr. to set up the appointment with his son for the next visit. I could not wait for that day, the big day. When it finally came up, I went to pick up my sister, then I stopped at home to get Père Noël. When we arrived there, everyone was waiting, including Grandpa. I introduced my parents and we sat. Then I told my parents that the reason they were there was to talk with Mr. Salomon on my behalf and to obtain the hand of Kettline, his daughter, for marriage. Both my godfather and my sister made a remarkable plea and portrayed me as one of the most reliable guys in the country. Since Mr. Salomon knew them both to begin with, he accepted my request to put Kettline on reserve for me. That was the best day of my life.

You remember that Mr. Salomon would not even sit properly to talk to me the first time? The second time was far better. He dressed nicely, invited his wife and his nephew, an Annapolis Naval Academy graduate, who at that time was a captain in the Haitian Navy, and a few other relatives. After the settlement, he ordered one of his servants to serve wine and finger foods to everybody. Then he introduced me as Kettline's fiancée. It was also a great victory for Grandpa.

The following day, Mr. Salomon Jr. began his investigation on me. One of the people he talked to was an old friend of mine, an ex-girlfriend who happened to be his acquaintance. She "scared the pants" off of him. She told him that, "Joel is the gentlest, most honest, respectable, and intelligent man in the neighborhood. However, when it comes to women, he is the sharpest and the fastest man on the block. He doesn't need to talk too much with them. They just follow him wherever he wants them to." I believe she was not the only person who described me like that. It was bad, very bad. I am pretty sure that Mr. Salomon did not go to his house from there. He went straight to his parents' house. He told Grandpa that he did not want Kettline to be with me anywhere without three chaperones, day or night. I did not need to worry about that. I knew that she was on "layaway," and I did not want to go anywhere else nor have anything to do with her, but seeing her at her house. I wanted her to have all of her time to concentrate on her studies. I rarely went out with her without the whole city with us, but I managed to steal few kisses from time to time.

Things were not always good for me, which is one of the reasons why I wrote this book. I am a survivor. Around six months after my official date of engagement, something terrible happened to me. I made a trip to the northern part of the country for pleasure. There, I decided to make a stopover at Joliette's parents' house to say "Hi" and to find out where she was. I met with them and spent some time visiting. As I was ready to leave, they asked me if I would carry something from them to her.

"Sure," I said. They gave me a small packet, her address, and her phone number. I had not seen her for almost two years. So that was the best way for me to make a comeback. Well, I delivered the packet and found a way to start a conversation with her. We talked about good times we had and times we missed. Remember in chapter three, I talked about how I met her and why I lost her. I lost her because of an inferiority complex. I thought that I was not going to do well and since she was in the medical school, I "split" in a cowardly way with her so I would not be an embarrassment to her. I honestly loved her. I loved her a lot. There was something about her that I could never explain. Seeing her again was like losing a treasure and finding it again.

I was facing the greatest challenge of my life, and I was going to have the toughest decision ever to make. I practically met Kettline and Joliette the same way and, as a matter of fact, I thought that God sent Kettline into my life as a second and last chance after I ran away from Joliette. So, Joliette and I began to get a little closer, but I did not want to hurt her another time, and I did not want to lose Kettline either.

One night it was Wednesday, October 17, 1979, I had a long conversation with Joliette, whom I sometimes called Jolie. We talked about the possibility of getting back together. If I am not mistaken, she had a boyfriend at that time that was also in the third year of medical school. I was a little bit nervous because I knew that I was going to marry Kettline, and that night was the only time since I met Kettline, that I felt I was vulnerable. That Wednesday, October 17, happened also to be my brother Jarman's birthday. I had a habit of calling him for his birthday, a habit that I keep to this date.

I set up a date with Jolie for the following day, Thursday, October 18, 1979, to go to a movie. I left her house very confused; I felt so trapped. I was not about to break the promise that I made to Kettline's parents and my parents, but I did not want to break Jolie's heart a second time. I told her that I was going to wish my brother "Happy Birthday," and I would see her tomorrow evening. I met with my brother Renel at his girlfriend's house and we left to pick up a friend of ours who used to work for a telephone company. The three of us went to a clinic where my older sister Edith was working. There my friend told me that he could help me to make the phone call to the U.S. free of charge. I asked him how. He told me that a friend of his who was working at the telephone company at that exact time would place the call for us. I accepted, and so it went. I spoke with my brother, wishing him "Happy Birthday" and talked to my folks as well. Edith also talked to her husband who was vacationing in New York.

On Thursday morning I went to work as usual. The office was downtown near the American Embassy. Around 9:30 a.m.

I left the office to pick up a diplomat from the airport that was coming from the States. Upon my return in the office, between about 1:30 and 2:30pm, someone told me that the director of the telephone company wanted to see me. I thought that he had a house for rent or lease because one of my responsibilities was to find houses for the diplomats that were living in Haiti for a long period. So, I called the gentleman who asked me if I had made a phone call to the U.S. the previous night. I said, "Yes, but why?"

He said that he would like to know who placed the phone call. I told him that I didn't know what he was talking about. He asked me to come see him after work because it was very important that he talk to me. Then he advised me that it was not only important that we talk, but it was a matter of straightening things out with the Haitian Government. And if I didn't cooperate, he would have me arrested. Man! I felt like I had been hit by a Mack truck. I was so scared that I had diarrhea instantly. I left the office and went straight home without telling anyone I was leaving. At home, I broke the news to my family. Everyone in the house started to cry. My sister Edith was there. Honest to God, she also got instant diarrhea too. I decided to go to the guy's office, but I was afraid to go by myself. So, I asked Kettline's cousin, an army captain, to go with me. It was hard for me to ask him because I was embarrassed, but I did not want to go alone.

In Haiti, anything is possible. Anyone with little or no authority can put you in jail with no questions asked. I explained the problem to the Captain who told me bluntly, "If they are going to arrest you, I won't be able to do anything for you." At that time I knew I was in deep trouble.

We went there anyway. As we entered the guy's office he said to me, "Mr. Esperance, I told you that I know you did not do anything wrong, I only want you to tell me who placed the phone call for you. You did not have to bring Captain Seïde with you, unless you know something that I don't know." I told him that I placed the phone call. Then he said, "In this case, you have used a false credit card to make the phone call. So, I would not have any choice but to report it to the American Embassy and to the police. And besides, the telephone company belongs to the Haitian Government, and Jean-Claude Duvalier (Baby Doc) is the owner."

Captain Seïde asked him to wait for a minute because he wanted to talk to me in private. Of course, I told him that a friend of mine placed the phone calls, and my friend told me that I would not have to pay a cent. The captain came back and told the director that I did not make the call. A friend of mine did it. The director told the captain that he knew who placed the call for me, but he wanted me to give the name of my friend as concrete evidence, so he could have him arrested.

My friend got fired because they suspected him of doing such, but they did not have clear evidence. They were investigating him. The director asked me if it were "Peter" (a fictitious name for my friend) who did it. I told him I preferred to talk to my cousin, the captain, and we would get back to him tomorrow. He asked me to bring a check for the amount that the phone call cost.

As I left the phone company, I told the captain that I would leave the country first thing in the morning. At that time, I already had my permanent American visa and I gave a 30-day notice of resignation to the service. I was at my last day of work. So, I said, I was not going to have to be arrested. The whole thing happened on the day that I was supposed to meet with Jolie. Unfortunately, I was not able to go out with her that night, and we did not have the chance to say goodbye. However, I went over to Kettline's house to break the news. They begged me not to leave the country. Kettline's father promised me that nothing would happen to me. I told them that I did not feel well and that I thought I was going to have a heart attack. They cried so much. Grandpa was so sad and Kettline was inconsolable. Before I left I reassured her that I was coming back to marry her. I left their house. I went to Renel's girlfriend's house. She worked for American Airlines and helped me to get a seat on Pan Am's first flight in the morning. Then I went home and told my folks that I was leaving the country early in the morning. There again it was like I had died. My folks spent the whole night crying.

On Friday, October 19, 1979, early in the morning, I boarded the first flight with Pan Am and left the country at 7:30 a.m., bound for Miami. I asked my brother Renel to call my workplace and let them know that I was sick and I had left the country for proper treatment. October 17, 1979, was the last time I saw Jolie. Still, I would have another chance to see her, but I would miss it, and the next time I would have a chance to ask for forgiveness, it would be twelve years later and by phone.

I went back to Haiti for the funeral of my father-in-law in May 1981. I met with her brother who told me that she knew I was in Haïti and that she wanted to see me. I went to the hospital to see her. Unfortunately, that was her last internship day. She had just left ten minutes before I showed up there. I felt bad because I wanted so much to apologize to her. She found out that I went there and had missed her. She went back to the hospital. I believe she talked to one of my sisters who did not tell her where she could find me. So, that was her third broken heart. According to some sources, she was so disappointed that she could not begin her residency until a year later. She basically lost a year of her schooling if I am not mistaken. I finally got a chance to see her face-to-face around December 2003. Unfortunately, I would not give details nor elaborate on this matter. I was so happy that I made the effort to see her. She was still very beautiful. She was happily married with her husband of twenty-three years and had two wonderful children. She never practices medicine. I don't think she really wanted to be a medical doctor. I think she was pushed by her parents, who were physicians themselves.

TWENTY-FIVE YEARS OLD TO TWENTY-SEVEN YEARS OLD

Living in New York

I arrived in Miami mid-morning, and I was so relieved. Although it was only an hour and twenty-five minute flight, it seemed to be a very long trip. I was so confused and frustrated about the fact that I was forced to leave Haïti; on the other hand, I called myself a very fortunate man, because if I had not had a permanent American visa, I would have had to face the unknown. Yes, maybe nothing would have happened to me. At the same time, I could have been arrested and put in jail. So, I had to wrestle with all of that. I definitely had mixed feelings. I was happy but sad at the same time. I was happy to make it to the U.S. because I had a big dream and only living permanently in the U.S. could make it possible. I was also happy that I was going to begin a new life.

I was sad because I left Kettline, my family, and my friends too soon. I wanted to spend at least one more month in Haïti.

The first thing I did in Miami was call my brother Jarman, informing him that I was there. He knew I was in Miami even before I told him. The phone company's director did in fact call their house in New York the night that I made the call there. Jarman had a suspicion that I was in trouble. So when I called home I asked him if he knew where I was. He answered, "Miami, and when will you be arriving in New York?" From Miami, I flew directly to Kennedy Airport. I believe I got to New York around 9 p.m. on the same night. My mom, Paul, Jarman, and Mary, Jarman's wife, came to pick me up at the airport. They took me to Nyack, where I was going to begin another new phase in my life.

The first two weeks in my new location were very boring. I was in a melancholic stage. I felt like I had lost everything. I missed the Haitian life. I had some difficulties getting acclimated to the new life. I missed Kettline the most. I had a picture of her that was taken in a park in New York at Coney Island Park when she visited the U.S. prior to my leaving Haïti. She took the picture and made it into a puzzle for me to put together. I put it together and carried it with me everywhere I went. I put the picture on the coffee table where everyone could see it when entering the main door of the house. It was a two story-house. The owner lived downstairs and we lived upstairs. The house had three bedrooms and there were seven of us living in it. A little bit after four weeks, I landed a job at a foundry; Chromalloy Sinter Cast Division in Nyack. The company was located about two miles away from where we lived. I would walk back and forth to work each day. I barely interviewed for an assistant Stock Keeper position. To my big surprise, I got the job. Right there they showed me where my office would be, and a nice hand-me-down desk was offered to me as well. My brother Jarman said that he couldn't believe that I was selected for that job. The company was a union shop. Because of that, I was hired as a temporary salary employee.

I made around $130.00 net average per week. I gave $100.00 a week to my mom to help her with the household budget.

As I said before, there was Mom, Dad, my brother Jarman and his wife, my brother Paul, my sister France, and me. Dad would always come and go from Haiti. My brothers and I were working steadily and my mom was working three or four half days a week. My mom was doing "day work." She cleaned houses for people. Some of the people she worked for were very kind and generous to her. One of them even helped her financially to bring some of us to the country.

My troubles in New York began like this. One of my friends, who was not a hardworking man and was constantly faking going to school but never went, came to pick me up at work almost every afternoon so we could go to Manhattan to have fun. My goals were to come and pursue my dream, which was to go back to Haïti after my studies to work as a diplomat for the U.S. government. Therefore, an American education was a must. So, I would take any chance that I could find to work toward my goals. I told my friend that I would rather have him drive me to school in the afternoons instead of going to Manhattan to have fun. My friend did not want to do that. It was more fun for him to go down there instead of taking me to school. Since I could not get a ride to go to school, I ended up in Manhattan almost every afternoon. I had to make a decision if I wanted to pursue an education. I decided to go back to Haïti to marry Kettline.

Anyway, I began to understand that living in the U.S.A. was not fun. Not only do people work very hard for their money, but also there were not many who would help you get ahead. I used to blame them, but after many years I came to realize that it was not their fault because they did not know any better. I also confirmed that my relatives who were here before worked their butts off while I was spending the money that they sent to us in Haïti unnecessarily. I felt so guilty.

My worst experience, or should I say the worst shocking moment while I lived in Nyack, NY was this: one morning, I did not go to work. I do not remember why I did not go. Anyway, I woke up that morning and it was snowing lightly and drizzling. Our house was right beside a major traffic road, Route 59, and there were a few businesses around. There was a factory right behind the house. I did work in that factory for six consecutive working days while I was on a temporary layoff. I took a look out the window. I saw a lady standing on the opposite side of the road, apparently waiting for a bus. I paid no attention to her and I went back to taking care of my business. Sometime later, I went back to the window for another peek. The woman was still standing there. I could see that she was somewhat wet and partially covered with snowflakes. She wrapped her handkerchief over her head and tied it under her chin. That time, I paid more attention to her and I started having visions in my head.

I said to myself: "Maybe she is going to work and she doesn't have a car or maybe she doesn't have kids to drive her to work." Then I began to think about my mom. "What if she were my mom, how sad I would feel." I really felt guilty. In a few more minutes, there was a bus approaching her. She changed positions to get closer to the sidewalk. She lifted her head to make a gesture to flag the bus down. To my biggest nightmare, the woman was indeed my mother. I almost had a heart attack. I tried to stop her from getting on the bus, but it was too late. I was extremely upset, furious in fact. I started screaming. I yelled at Paul and Jarman, who had just come back from work. I told them what happened and I asked them why they did not make arrangements for Mom to go to work and to pick her up from work. They told me that it was not their fault and they would not want her to do that, but this was life in the big city. I cried so much that I fell asleep. I found out where Mom was working that day. I borrowed one of their cars to go pick her up. Since that day, every time my mom had to work I would wait for one of my brothers to come back from work so I could get the car to take my mom to work. Then I would come back home, drop the car off, and walk to work. I would take late lunches so I could go home, get a car to get her from work, bring her home and go back to work. When I realized that was putting a heavy load on me, I decided to use a different strategy.

I wanted to stay faithful to Kettline. I did not want to go out with anyone else. There were a number of young ladies in the church where I fellowshipped. Nevertheless, I got tempted. I decided to chat with some of those that were more or less appealing to me. In the beginning, I did not want to pay too much attention to them. I was playing "Mr. Cool Guy." One lady in particular, whom I will call Idalia, was more jovial than the others seemed to be, and I knew that she had a brand new car and was working second shift. That was the perfect match. I said to my self, if it works, I would take her to and pick her up from work and then I would take her home and keep the car. Idalia and I became good friends and I started to hang out with her more and more, take her places, then to and from work, and finally she asked me to keep the car at nights. Guess what? It worked. In the morning I used the car to take Mom to work, went to work myself, picked Mom up from work, and went back to work. In the afternoon, I took Idalia to work, went to school, then picked her up and took her home. She was happy, and I was happy.

As time went by, we began to take the friendship to another level, which was not the plan. I thought it was the time to make things right. I told her about Kettline, and I also told her that I would marry Kettline in the near future. One good thing, I never lied to anyone about having a fiancée. She took it well and life continued. One night we were sitting in her car in a park having a conversation when suddenly a policeman came right up behind our car and activated his flashing lights. I was new in the states. I did not know that you don't get out of your car when you get pulled over by police until you are asked to. So, I quickly opened the car door and was about to get out.

Idalia screamed, "Don't get out of the car! You will get shot!"

At the same time, the officer yelled, "Stay in the car!"

I panicked. I thought I was going to get killed. She assured me that it was going to be okay. Then she said, "The worst thing that can happen is that we will get a warning. But more likely, he will ask us to get out of here." She was right. The officer asked to see my driver license and the car registration. I showed him my license, and Idalia showed him the car registration. He looked at them and told us that the park was not there for people to "hang out" after hours. He gave us back the papers and asked us to leave the park.

I made a comeback to a lady that I had met a few months beforewhile I was still living in Haiti. To honor her privacy, I will call this particular woman Sofia. She was in Haiti on a business trip from New York. There, I met with her per the request of a mutual friend; I drove her around and ran some errands for her as well. Shortly after, she went back to Haiti and we met again. Since we knew each other it did not take long for us to hang out, and that time it was different. We had a pretty good time in Haiti.

She was not broke. She left some money for me in Haiti and sent some to me till I left Haiti. I placed a phone call to her, which was well received. The following day, we were already together. As I mentioned a while ago, I was giving $100 a month to my mom. So I didn't have enough left for my expenses. She knew I had just come and that I was helping my folks. She did not only help financially, but would buy things that I needed. My parents thought that Sofia was only a good friend of mine and that she was being generous. I kept that relationship going for a while. Once again, I talked to her about Kettline and made it clear that I would marry Kettline soon and that after we married I would never have those types of relations with anyone; a promise that I kept.

I knew that what I was doing was not right and certainly not right to Kettline, but I did not have much of a choice. So I thought at that time. I rationalized my gross behavior as follows: I needed some money to buy a car, and the only way at that time I could manage was to ask Sofia for help. I would not want anyone to call me a "gigolo," for that I was not. She was doing things for me from her heart or because I helped her in Haiti. I met another Haitian, whom I will call Yvette, one of my brother's friends' nieces. I said "another Haitian" because Idalia and Sofia were Haitians. Yvette and I had some good times. We both were new in the states and had almost the same background. We enjoyed talking with each other, but for some reason, she thought our relationship was to go further. Since the first time I saw Kettline, I knew I was going to marry her.

Anyway, there was a gentleman, whom I called Willie, in the neighborhood. He was very "slick" and had more money than all the average young men in the area. The guy, to my knowledge, never worked hard for a living. I was told that he worked for a few months upon his arrival in the U.S.A. and then he was involved in a car accident, which ended his need to work. In the seventies, when someone had a car accident and was not at fault, that person could get pretty healthy cash as compensation. So that gentleman had a good case and ended up with, according to what I have been told, more than $750,000. Girls were fighting over the dude.

One time I went over to Yvette's house and the dude was there. I did not go in right a way, I waited for a while, and then I went in. She did not want to talk to me, so I left. Later on, I called her and asked her if I could come see her. She said that it was okay. I went there and, to my big surprise, she told me that she could no longer see me. I asked why. She told me it's because I was engaged to a girl that I left in Haiti and that she was the only girl that I would be married to, and I did not need her. She did not want to tell me who told her all of that. I knew automatically that Willie told her about my private business. That was the way the gentleman operated. Next thing I knew, he was dating Yvette and I was completely out of the picture.

Second encounter with the police

My second encounter with the police in the U.S. was a frightening experience, and as of today, I still get goose bumps talking about it. I was taking English-as-a-Second-Language at Nyack Public High School at nights. Usually, I used one of my brothers' cars or Idalia's, but that particular night a friend of mine dropped me at the school with the condition that Jarman would pick me up. Well, Jarman and his wife, Mary, drove Paul's car, a brand new yellow Camaro, to pick me up. On our way home, Jarman wanted to buy a sub sandwich so he could eat something prior to getting home. So from the school, since I was driving, Jarman asked me to make a stop at a sub shop on Broadway. A few blocks down from the sub shop was Paul's girlfriend's house. Next to the house was a gas station and there was a public phone right across. We stopped right in front of the telephone booth to make a phone call to check if Paul was over at his girlfriend's home. (She is now his wife.) While I was making the call, Jarman and Mary sat in the car. Suddenly, Jarman spotted a police cruiser parked at the gas station facing the telephone booth, and at the time he realized that the officer turned his bright light toward them in the car. Jarman made a motion with his hand and asked me to hurry up. I immediately ran out, got in the car, and took off. The minute we left, the police drove right behind us. We made a stop at a stop sign, and he stayed right behind us. When we took off, he also took off and remained behind us. Jarman began to get panicky. He asked me to slow down and maintain a steady speed. We were in a residential area and in just a few hundred meters there was a four-way stop. We proceeded very carefully toward the next stop sign and then we stopped. After we stopped, we moved toward the next stop sign, which was also a four-way stop. As we were about to stop, there were already three police cruisers, with one at the end of street facing the center area of the corner. And there was another cruiser behind the one that was right behind us. The officer right behind us activated his warning lights.

Jarman said, "Oh, my God! What in the world did Paul do?" Then, the officer ordered me to pull over. At that point we also realized that there were two policemen in the cruiser behind. One of the officers in the cruiser behind us got out of the cruiser and asked for the passenger, Jarman, on the right of the driver to step out of the vehicle. I remember that Jarman said, "What in the world has Paul gotten himself into now?"

As I mentioned, there were three police cruisers, one from each corner. The officer who was on the opposite corner from us also got out of his cruiser with a shotgun in his hand and yelled, "The gentleman sitting on the passenger side, please put your hands behind your head and step out of the car." I thought he was talking to me, so I was about to get out of the car when Jarman told me that they were talking to him. He asked me to stay in the car. As my brother came out of the car, he was ordered to lean toward the front of the car and spread his legs. So all the time Jarman was outside, I had my hand behind my head inside of the car. Mary, Jarman's wife was very frightened in the back seat. All the police officers drew their revolvers or shotguns and pointed at Jarman's head. The officer who ordered him to step out of the car walked slowly toward him. As that officer got closer, the others moved closer also. The officer pushed Jarman's head toward the hood of the car and began to search him. They were looking for a handgun or other weapons.

All the time that the officers were dealing with Jarman, I kept my hand behind my head because I did not know what was going on. I was stunned. I thought that we were going to be killed. I heard the officer ask Jarman where he was an hour ago. Jarman told him that he was at home and left home a half-hour ago to pick me up from the school. Then the officer asked him for an identification card. Jarman gave him his driver's license. At that time Jarman had an Ohio driver's license. The officer took a look at it and said to Jarman, "We are looking for a gentleman who just robbed a house at gunpoint in the Spring Valley area." The description that we got matches your profile. We are sorry for the inconvenience. If you want to bring a complaint, you may do so." He gave Jarman his police card and a number to call in case Jarman wanted to. Then they left. Guess what, I could no longer drive the car. My legs were numb. It took me a good ten minutes after the fact before I could start the car and go home.

First full night out–Last whipping:

Let me tell you about my last whipping and my first full night out. I was twenty-six years old. On a beautiful Saturday evening, one of my friends, Ederns, came to pick me up to go to a party in Queens, NY. Although my friend came to pick me up in a car, I found out that we were to get another ride to the party. At that time my friend did not have a car of his own and neither did I. Anyway, I hopped in the car where I met another friend of his. We drove for a while; left that car and someone else came to get us and drove us to the party. To my biggest surprise, I met one of my old girlfriends, whom I call Wilma, at the party. Can you imagine having only been in the country for five or six months and you go to a party in another city where you have never been before? Meeting that girl was like a Godsend. I firmly believe that I had more fun at that party than any other guest. Sometime around three in the morning, Wilma told me that it was time for her to leave, and that she would want me to take her home, somewhere in Manhattan. I asked the friend who drove us to the party if he could take us to Manhattan. He did not want to. So I decided to go anyway. My friend Ederns and I took a train with Wilma, and I believe with two other ladies that came to the party with her. We got there sometime around 4:30 a.m., and by the time we managed to get back to Queens, it was six in the morning, only to find out that our friend was long gone and had left us behind.

Neither Ederns nor I had money for transportation. We put our minds together to come with a strategy that could take us back to Nyack. We tried to phone a few friends to come to pick us up. Not a Fat Chance! Instead, we lost the last fifty cents we had. By the way, a telephone call cost only ten cents at that time. We became very desperate. We came up with a stupid idea that would work for us. We were to find some Haitians and ask them for a few bucks so we could take a train and buses to go back home. What was the idea? It was targeting black passersby's who had some Haitian's traits. We would cuss his or her mom by saying dirty words in Créole.

One would ask, "Why did you have to cuss black passersby's, especially cussing their moms?" If you want to get a Haitian in rage, just cuss his or her mom. Let me explain why. In the slavery days, Haitian slaves were brutally mistreated by the French Colons. They took great pleasure giving Latin or Greek names to their slaves. The Colons not only treated them badly, but also brutally raped their mothers, wives, and daughters. Of course, no one takes pleasure in seeing or finding out that someone close to them is getting raped. When something like that happened, it was the most horrible thing that could happen to a slave or his entire family. So, when a slave was extremely mad with another slave and wanted to hurt his feelings, or insult him, he would say to him in Créole, *"co languete menmenw"* dirty words, which could be translated in a very vulgar way in English. I believe that it is even worse when someone that you already hate did that to your loved ones.

As I said before, every time we spotted a black person passing we would repeat those words loud enough that we could catch the person's attention. If they were Haitian they would understand that we were calling on their compassion as a fellow countryman. After a few attempts we were lucky to find ourselves with enough cash to get home. When I finally got home it was 9:00 a.m. One of my brothers, Paul, told me that Mom was very upset due to the fact that I was not home when she checked my room. In spite of the warning I managed to get in and I laid flat on the bed as if I had been there all the time. A few minutes later, I started to make some noise to let Mom know I was there. I had not been even two minutes in the room before Mom showed up. She did not ask me where I had been or where I spent the night. She started to beat up on me with one of her sandals. Then, she picked up a piece of wood that was around the bed and began to beat my head with the rod. All that time she blocked the door. Our culture does not allow us to hold our parents' hands when they are putting a whipping on us, nor block their hands. I had to use a quick maneuver to get out of the room. I am not kidding you. I got a real whipping that day. Not only was it my last whipping, but the way and the condition under which I received it makes it unforgettable. I usually tell my boys that if my mom could put a "whoop" on me at the age of twenty-six, they would not be exempt from one until they are forty or until they get married, whichever comes first.

TWENTY-SIX YEARS OLD TO THIRTY-FIVE YEARS OLD

Embarking toward the Marriage Life

I was about to enter a new phase in my life. I was going back to Haiti to get married to Kettline. Before I could do that, I had to disconnect myself with Idalia and Sofia. It wasn't easy. First, I called Idalia and told her that it was time that we terminated the relationship. The reason I said it in that way was for the fact that in the beginning, I told her that I was engaged to Kettline and that I would go back to marry her in the following year. Unfortunately, she didn't think that I would go back to marry a woman in Haiti while I was living in NY. Most guys who left girls behind never went back to marry them. So it was Idalia's nightmare to digest the fact that I wanted to do so. She asked me to change my mind. I told her that if I did that I would never be able to go back to Haiti without being arrested and even being killed. I told her that Kettline had so many high-ranked military people in her family, and a few Tonton Macoutes (Boogey men), and that Kettline was the only girl in the family. Those guys wouldn't hesitate to get me arrested and throw me in jail. She said to me: "Let's go to Canada for a few years and after that you could apply for American citizenship. Being an American, no one would be able to hurt you." I told her that it was easier said than done. After a few weeks of debating, I won the battle. She was upset, but she made it clear that upon my return we would continue the relationship. I told her that it was not the right thing to do. And that was the way we left it. I have to say that it was not the end of my troubles.

Next, it was time to talk to Sofia. I thought that it was going to be easy, but unfortunately I was wrong. Sofia got very furious when I told her that I was going to get married. She asked me: "Did you hit your head? Have you suffered a concussion, or are you out of your mind? How come you want to go to Haiti to marry a little girl that hasn't even finished her secondary education?" What she didn't understand, and did not want to understand, was the fact that I told her at the beginning that our friendship was only going to be a friendship, because I would have to marry Kettline. The same as Idalia, she asked me not to break our friendship indefinitely. After a few weeks I made a phone call to Kettline's dad to let him know that I wanted to come to Haiti to get married and to ask Kettline to set up a date. Kettline and her parents set a date that was approximately three months from the time I made the phone call. August 2, 1980 was the wedding date My father in-law told me that I wouldn't have to buy anything but my suit and a pair of shoes because he wanted to do everything and he wanted to throw a big party for the wedding. I bought Kettline a ring and she bought me one. Within our thirty years of marriage she changed her ring twice and mine once. I took my father in-law's offer; I rented two tuxedoes and bought two pairs of shoes; one for my brother Renel and one for myself. Renel was the best man at my wedding; at that time he was still living in Haiti. I left NY one week before the wedding day. Besides my family, one of my friends went to Haiti with me. I was stunned. I found out that Kettline's family was embarking on a mission to give their daughter one of the biggest weddings in Haiti. We had two sets of bridesmaids and ushers and large number of flower girls. They rented a party room at one of the largest hotels in the country for the reception and we spent our honeymoon in that hotel as well.

Let's go straight to the day–the big day–the wedding day. First, I made Kettline upset. One of my friends, who was in the wedding party, decided to pull himself out at the last minute. Kettline didn't want him in the party to begin with, but because of me she had accepted him. It took me a while to find someone else to replace him. I wanted to give the wedding an American flare; I asked the same friend of mine that pulled out from the wedding party to decorate the car we were going to use after we got married. The wedding time was set for 6:30 p.m. Please bear in mind, it was in summer, which means it was daytime savings period. My brother, who wanted to wear the tuxedo so much, had been dressed since 3:30 p.m. He made sure that I got dressed at 4:30 p.m. and we decided to walk around so people could see us. I believe that I was one of the few people who got married in a tuxedo in Haiti; besides the military officers who most of the time got married in a tuxedo style of uniform.

It was a hot day to begin with, and despite that, I had two glasses of wine because I was so nervous and anxious. I walked two miles away to one of my sister's house. Can you imagine wearing a tuxedo in 90-degree weather, walking for four miles back and forth, while having two glasses of wine in your system? Yes, that was my situation a few hours before I got married. Kettline was supposed to ride to the church with her parents and I was supposed to ride in the decorated car with my close friends. People were looking at us, wondering why we got dressed like that. Some of them thought that we were high-ranked military guys. There were quite a few ladies who could not believe that I was getting married. Some of them predicted that the wedding would not last for three months, some predicted one year, and some a couple years.

They were standing around to see how I was going the get in the church. Upon arriving at the church's parking lot, there were already a massive number of people gathering around the church wondering what was going on. There were approximately five hundred people around the church, partly because of the tuxedoes that we wore, and partly because Belony Salomon's daughter was getting married. I was also well known in the areas of the church. As a means of security, we had a number of policemen and a few boy scouts' troops. Renel was to be escorted into the church by policemen. I have to admit that I was scared for a while. A few minutes later, Kettline had arrived with her folks. I could not wait to see her. Coincidently, we were getting married in the same church that we met. I was thinking, *I can not believe that two plus years ago, I came to this church, after I first saw Kéké, just to see her. And, a friend of mine would not let me see or talk to her. Now, here I am standing impatiently to receive her as my bride.* Is that something? There came the most beautiful bride in the world. She walked in with finest and firm as she was escorted by her proud Dad. Her wedding gown was fascinating and outstanding. Overall, she was spectacular that evening. The ceremony began right away. There were four pastors presiding over the wedding ceremony. Professional cameramen were all around the sanctuary and the reception areas. Unfortunately, we did not have a great set of wedding pictures. We had to salvage a few good ones to make an album. Besides the pictures, a strange thing happened: the senior pastor mistakenly inserted the ring on the right finger, but the wrong hand. I tried to switch it; he insisted that it was okay. If you take a look at my wedding pictures, you will see that in most of them I had my wedding ring on the wrong hand.

The ceremony was long but wonderful. It was very difficult to get out of the church, because of the amount of people who gathered in the front. Those people were not invited and the worst part was that they found out where the reception was going to be, and most of them went and got inside of the hotel anyway. The church was approximately three miles from the hotel so the people ran as fast as the wedding cortege. Please note: the road's condition was not good and there were so many people that it was difficult for the cars to maneuver among the people. I am sorry to say that it was a mess; about two hundred people were invited and there were approximately three hundred inside of the hotel. It was not unusual in Haiti to have a lot of wedding crashers. They call them *"Dassaumen"*; in Créole, it sounds close to "assault men," except they don't mug or beat up people. They just ate and drank what they could get their hands on. Although there were police officers and boy scouts, they couldn't stop people from ransacking the food. My father in-law asked the people who were not invited to leave immediately on a Public Address (PA) system, or he would have to use force. You remember what I said about my in-laws, they were very powerful and well known in Haiti. So, five to ten minutes after the announcement, the place was in order. Then he said, "Let the fun continue." It was a lavish reception and at the end of the affair, my father in-law invited everyone, who wanted to, to go to his private disco club to continue the party till dawn. That meant food and drink, which included alcoholic beverages. My parents and Kettline's parents stayed for a little while to make sure that everything was okay. And we went on to begin our honeymoon. We were to spend three days there, but we ended up staying four or five days extra due to the fact that there was a bad tornado a couple of days after the wedding. There was one sad thing that happened in the affair; Grandpa Salomon was not able to participate in the ceremony or the reception because he was hospitalized. He had prepared a speech for our wedding, it was so sad that he could not give the speech himself, but he asked Colonel Seïde, one of Ket tline's close cousins to make the speech on his behalf. We kept his speech in one of our wedding albums.

Kettline and I left the hotel on Thursday. I was to leave the country on Saturday afternoon, so Ketlline's parents invited me to stay at their house for the next two nights. Something strange happened on the first night. They wanted me to sleep in Kettline's bedroom. Why do I say something strange happened if I only had to sleep in Kettline's bedroom? You remember that I said that Kettline lived with her grandparents. So her bedroom was between her two grandparents. There was no direct entrance into her room, but through one of the grandparent's bedrooms. That means they were not sharing the same bedroom. I felt very uncomfortable to sleep right next to them with their grandchild. I refused to do it. Kettline did not have a problem to sleep with her new husband, but I spent the next two nights sleeping alone. My plan was to leave my wife in Haiti so she could finish her secondary school and then join me in the following years in the U.S.A. Her Dad did not like that idea, and besides, that was going to be a load of responsibilities for him. He wanted me to leave with her right away. He promised to help me out financially while I would be continuing my education. I left the country on the following Saturday, eight days after I got married, alone. On the following Saturday, I met with Sofia who wanted to discuss how we were going to manage to remain friends. Surprisingly, I denied her request and her deal. Grandpa got better in the middle of the month, August 1980, and decided to take a trip to the U.S. He would not leave Kettline behind, so he took the full responsibility to bring my brand new wife to me. They came at the end of the month of August. I met them at the airport and took them to one of their relatives in the Brooklyn area. There I met with the family, some I knew and some that I had not met before. We had a small family reception and Grandpa handed Kettline's hand to me and said, "Married people do not live apart, I personally bought your wife to you." Then he handed me a bag of cash that he had been saving for a while. He added, "It may not be much, but it will help you to get on your feet." I thanked him and I invited him to meet with the rest of my relatives, who couldn't go to the wedding in Haiti. Let's just say, I was no longer a free man anymore.

At the beginning, it was tough to get adjusted to married life. Our life in New York was very difficult; we lived with my parents in a three-bedroom house. My mom and my sister France slept in one bedroom, since my dad lived in Haiti most of the time. My brother Jarman slept in one bedroom with his newly wedded wife, and my brother Paul slept in the other bedroom. So that left Kettline and me to sleep in the living room on a sofa bed. If you remember some time ago, I mentioned that Kettline had her own bedroom at home, and now was sleeping in a living room on a sofa bed. What a transition Kettline wanted to live as a married woman, while I wanted to continue to live as a "Playboy" after we got married. In her first few weeks, something stupid happened: The telephone rang. Kettline picked it up and answered, "This is Mrs. Joel Esperance. Who do you want to talk to?" The caller responded, "Who did you say you were?" Kettline said, "Je suis la femme de Joël." "Est ce que je peux parler à Joël," the caller asked. At that time, Kettline began to get irritated. She asked the caller to identify herself. The caller told her that it did not matter, because Joel knew who she was. Kettline said, "In this case, you are not going to talk to Joel, period." The caller replied, "My name is Idalia, and I am coming to kick your butt." I was sitting in the dining room with Kettline and my mom, and I told Kettline that when the woman shows up not to pay any attention to her.

Approximately ten minutes later Ms. Idalia arrived at the doorstep. "Where is Kettline?" she asked. Kettline answered, I am upstairs. The house that we lived in was a two-story home, so we were on the top floor. Most of the time, the downstairs door was always opened. Idalia came and met with Kettline at the door. Kettline told her that she was not going to let her in. Idalia told her that the house belongs to Mrs. Joel Esperance Sr., (My mom). My mom interjected, "The boys pay the rent. So, since Joel is one of the persons that pays the rent, the house belongs to Kettline as well." Then Kettline told her not to come back again. I was so scared; I thought that Idalia was going to really put a whoop on Kettline. I went into hiding in Paul's bedroom. I began to leave Kettline at home with my mom while I went out with the gang. You can easily tell that our marriage life was not on the right track. Sofia did not want to give me a chance. So, I started to get very upset; my stress level was increasingly getting higher. Early in October 1980, Jarman, who used to live in Cleveland, Ohio, went back there to work for an Aircraft parts manufacturing plant, and called to ask me if I wanted to come to Cleveland to work. I quickly said yes. The president of the company was looking for a metallographer (Metallurgical Technician) to open a new laboratory. At that time, I was working as a lab tech at Chromalloy Sintercast Division in West Nyack. I had less than a month in that position. Jarman asked me if would be able to set up the metallurgical laboratory for the president. I told him, "With no doubt."

On October 17, 1980, Jarman's birthday, I was on a plane going to Cleveland, Ohio. I left Kettline with my mom and my family. Maybe you are saying I finally left her behind as I always wanted to do. No, it was solely for our own good. You will see that clearly in the following chapters. It wasn't going to be easy, but at the end we will be doing well.

Even though I had to fight a few more battles, I can say that I also had a lot of fun during those early years. I thought I was going to work by myself; I was very worried. Then I found out that there was a chemical engineer, Richard Philippe, who was going to work with me. Or should I say, that I was going to work for. I did well and I began to grow; things were getting better and better. The company was brand-new and did not have a big allowance for the lab, so Richard and I bought all equipment used. I have learned so much from him, and we did travel quite a few times to visit other laboratories. Eight years later, I would name my second son after him. One of my ridiculous experiences was in early 1982. Richard asked me to order some glassware for the lab. Among the tests that we conducted in the lab, one was "titration" and one of the instruments we used for the test was a "burette," which is a glass tube with measurements marked on the side and a stopcock at the bottom to release an accurately measured quantity of liquid. Among the glassware that I had to order were a few stopcocks. In order for you to understand what I am about to tell you, I have to set it up well. Most foreigners, when speaking English, have the tendency to speak backward, especially the French. So, I used to call the stopcock, "cock stopper" or "stopping cock." I hope you understand. Here it goes: I called the vendor's phone, a woman answered, "How may I help you?" I said, "My name is Joel, I would like to buy a few cock stoppers. Do you have some?" She hung up the phone. I called her back and asked her the same question. That time she called me "pervert." I was shocked, because I did not know why someone would call me pervert for asking for a lab instrument. I went to my boss's office and told him what had happened. He said, "Oh my, no way." He put his hand in front of his mouth, and he asked, "Did you tell who asked you to call the order?" I said, "No, I just gave her my name." Then he said, "Thank you Jesus." I asked him if I said something bad. He told me because of my accent and the fact that I said the word backward it sounded real bad. He did not tell me what it sounded like. What I did not tell you was that my boss's nickname was Dick.

It took me almost a year to find out what the lady thought I said. I met one of my good friends at the company, a friend that fits the genuine definition of what a true friend is. Even today, I still can say she is a good friend of mine. Let me tell you a little bit about her. Her name is Suzanne. One day, the president and owner of the company told me that he was going to give me some help in the lab. At that time, I was working a lot of hours. I thanked him and let him know that I would appreciate any help. The following Monday he introduced a gorgeous young woman and said, "Joel, this is Suzanne. She is going to work with you in the metallurgical lab." At that time, I was pretty much in charge of the metallurgical laboratory. Suzanne was the president's daughter, newly wedded and second child. Besides being gorgeous, she was extremely coquettish, and had the finest and most delicate march. First, I thought that she would not want to work and if that would have been the case, I wouldn't have been able to do a thing about it. Part of the job was to section parts for metallurgical examination preparation. We used a "wet cut off" machine to section the parts. During that operation, there would be a heavy fume and smell released from the machine. That operation was so bad that one-day, after spending few hours cutting parts, I went to a supermarket to buy groceries. While I was standing in the cashier line, I heard someone say, "Something is burning." And people started looking around. I knew that it was me, but I did not say anything. Second, she had beautiful and naturally long fingernails; she would not want to mess them up. Anyway, I started to train her on the cut off machine. We worked for a few hours and I asked her if she wanted to take a break. She told me that she would not take break until lunchtime. At lunch, I told her that I would see her later. She stayed in the laboratory and had lunch by herself. For the first two weeks I spoke with her only if there was something to do with work. One day, she asked me if I would not mind having lunch with her in the lab. I said I wouldn't mind. That was how we became good friends. By the way, she was the one who explained to me what the lady thought I said when I asked for the "Cock Stopper."

Suzanne and I had developed a good working relationship. Her family and mine got together frequently, and sometimes her father would invite me to have lunch with them. That was a pretty good perk. While she was working there, her dad sold the company to a major Investment Castings business; their headquarters were in Chicago. Her dad remained president and general manager of the company. Those years were great. While I was at work, I believe it was around May of 1984, I got a phone call from home; Kettline, then pregnant, was bleeding. Suzanne offered to drive me home, but I declined. I drove myself home. When I got there, Kettline was very scared. Anyone would be able to detect that. She told me that she did not know what happened; she was just taking a shower when she realized there was a good amount of blood in the bathtub. I told her that we needed to call her doctor; the doctor asked us to come into the clinic right away. So we did. The doctor did not waste any time, she asked us to go straight to the hospital and wait for her. A few hours later, we got the bad news. The baby was dead in her womb. Kettline was administered some types of medication to help her deliver on her own. The baby was a boy. After that miscarriage, we were so devastated. I took sometime off of work so that I could be with her. A couple months later, I took Kettline to Florida as a way of disconnecting ourselves from the usual activities. Meanwhile, things were not going well at the company; as a result, the president left unexpectedly. I remember this vividly. Suzanne got a phone call from her dad telling her about the news. She burst out crying, saying, "It is not fair, it is not fair." I asked her what happened; she would not tell me. I was very confused. I never saw her upset like that, and besides, she was weeping inconsolably. I was upset because of the fact that she was and I did not know what had made her so sad. We really were like brother and sister. I called her "My Italian Sis." She called me her "Haitian Bro." Finally, she told me that her dad got upset and left and that she also would leave right away. There was no way that she would spend another hour in the company. Suzanne told me to walk her out. In the parking lot, we held each other for a long time. We both wept like two babies. I never knew that we were so attached until that day. She left and I went back inside; I continued to cry. She lived, at that time, about twenty-five minutes from the plant, and by the time she got to her house she had called me two times. I spent the next couple months very sad. It was like I was mourning the loss of a close relative. Suzanne was and is even today, a good and true friend to me. I still have great respect and consideration for her father. For the rest of my life, I will be grateful and thankful to him and his family.

Later that year, 1984, Kettline and I met our first Haitian friend in Ohio, a big, tall man named Lucrece Mio. It was Wednesday, November 1984, the day before Thanksgiving. I came back from work and Kettline told me that someone called and wanted to talk to me. Then she said the person who called told her that he was Haitian, and that he had been in the Cleveland area for a while. I told Kettline that the gentleman was "pulling her leg." She told me that I might be right because he spoke French with an American accent. Anyway, I called the phone number that he left for me to call. A woman answered the phone and I quickly realized that she was an American. At that time, I perceived that the gentleman was not Haitian. I asked to speak with Mr. Mio. He came on the phone. I said, "Monsieur Mio, Je suis Joël Espérance. Comment allez-vous."

"Très bien merci," he responded.

I continued, "Ma femme m'a dit que vous êtes Haïtien et vous vivez ici à Cleveland."

"Bien Sur," he answered. I picked the accent, and I wanted to be sure that he was Haitian, I asked him in Créole, "Dépi ki lè ou icite?.(How long have you been here?)

"A peu près un an et demi." (About a year and a half)

So we continued to talk in Creole. From there I invited him to eat with us on Thursday, which was Thanksgiving. He accepted the invitation. He came home on the following day and he also brought two other Haitian friends with him. They were Renee and Felix. The following Sunday, he took the liberty to take us to visit the Gaujean's family, Max and Emmelyne. Then we met a few other Haitians. Even today, we have a small but strong Haitian community in the northeast; the Cleveland, Akron, and Toledo areas. Max was the Dean of the Haitian community.

Major development in our lives

On December 22 or 23, 1985, Kettline and I bought our first home in Painesville, Ohio. We have a picture of that house framed in our office. I did not think that we could purchase the house at the time. Since I was hooked on photography, I took a picture of the house with the "for sale" sign in the front. I said that in the event that I did not buy the home, I would give the picture as a gift to whoever did buy it. I framed it and waited for a month or two to put an offer on the house. Not only was the offer accepted, but also we got a loan and we moved in. Kettline and I were taking a few college courses at Lakeland Community College while we were still working some long hours. There was no question about it, my life took a serious and troublesome turn. The new friends that I met were all, with the exception of one, professionals. They were doctors (MD), engineers, professors, pharmacists, and preachers to name a few. At one time, one of my co-workers, an engineer, asked me if I had a college degree. I said, "I don't have a college degree, but I have a baccalaureate certificate." I wish I did not have to say that, because it took me almost an hour to explain my educational background. After all, the gentleman told me point blank, "You don't have a college degree, period." Then he asked me if anyone in my family had a "real" college degree. I said, "No." I felt so bad. What I did not know was in less than ten years, all but one of us would hold at least one college degree. Praise the Lord!

Please remember that I said "In less than 10 years" that means I went through hell to get my education while already married, with two children, and a full-time job.

Unexpected raise on the job and graceful addition to the family

I was a Metallurgical Laboratory Supervisor; the department manager hired a technician to work with me. The technician reported directly to me. Since I am the kind of person that is always open with everyone, I happened to have a conversation with a young engineer, by the name of Marco, about the technician while we were having lunch. By the way, Marco is actually the president of a major company in Houston, Texas. During the course of our conversation, a sensitive subject came up. We began to talk about salary, where I told Marco about how much money I was making at that time. Marco told me that he wanted to tell me something that must be kept confidential. I said, "Okay." He told me that the technician that worked for me was making X-amount of money over of what I was making. I asked him how he found out what she was making. He told me that he had opened her check by mistake. Marco at that time was working for the same manager that I reported to. By the time we were having that conversation, there was already a management restructure. Our manager had been removed from his position and replaced temporarily by a Senior Quality Control Engineer. I did not want to waste time; I spoke with the acting manager. Instead of him helping me out, he went to find out for himself. He went and asked for more money. For some reason, he came back and told me that he was no longer going to be my boss, and Neo, a staff member and engineering manager, would be my new boss. Neo was also a good friend of mine at the time. Soon after, I got a phone call from Neo who asked me to tell him about what I found out and how. I told him that my technician was making X-amount of money more than what I was making and since I knew I could trust him, I told him how I found out. He said. "If it is true she is making more money than you, I will let you know." In the same afternoon, I got myself an increase, of the X-amount +Y-amount. Oh, my goodness, gracious, that mishap worked to my advantage. During my tenure in that position, I had a chance to visit a few companies, such as Pratt & Whitney, General Electric, in Cincinnati, Ohio and Lynn, Massachusetts. I developed great working relationships with their key employees.

In spring 1986, Kettline and I were having a disagreement and she did want to talk with me. Most of the time after we had a fall out, she would not speak with me for a couple of days and sometimes, a week. That particular time, I could not take it any longer, so I started to talk to her. After a while, she broke down in tears and she told me that she was pregnant. First, I could not believe it, but she assured me that it was true. That was the biggest news I have ever received in my entire life. As I explained earlier in this chapter, we lost our first baby through a miscarriage. Since then we had been trying to have another baby. Kettline was taking a number of fertility pills; I had done all kinds of tests to determine if we could have another chance. I am not kidding with you when I said that we had tried everything, everything that friends and family told us to. We were so happy, and we began to make plans. After one and a half months, Kettline went to see her doctor for a check-up. The doctor immediately ordered her to stop working for extra precaution. At the time, she was also ordered not to have intercourse under any circumstances if we wanted to have the baby. That did not bother me at all; I was just focused on my future baby. On her three months' check up, the doctor put her on bed rest, and she was supposed to see the doctor every two weeks. On her five months' check up, she went under a minor surgery to stitch her cervix. February 14, 1987, Kettline gave birth to a wonderful baby boy. I called almost everyone I knew all over the world to let them know that we had our first child. Kettline and I were thinking about having her grandma, whom she called Mom, come into the U.S. to be godmother of our child. Unfortunately, on January 10, 1987, Grandma passed away. As I explained earlier in the book, Kettline had lived with her grandparents since she was a couple months old and she had a miscarriage previously. This is to say because she had a difficult pregnancy, it was not an easy task to tell her about her Grandma's death. I decided, and also was advised by her doctor and our family, not to tell her. Besides, I was living in constant fear wondering if Kettline was going to make it through that time, and then came that news. You don't really want to know what kind of life I was living. As Kettline was getting closer to her delivery time, the more she wondered why it took so long before I could pick up her Mom from the airport. I had never lied to Kettline before, and then I found myself lying to her every time she asked about her Grandma's visit to the U.S. I knew that it was going to be so painful for her. About six months after we got married, her grandpa died and about six months after her grandpa's death, her father died. We wanted so much to have her grandma to be able to see our first child. God did not plan it that way. It was at the end of February 1987, two weeks after our son, Joel Joseph (Joey) was born that I told Kettline about Grandma's death. It was probably one of her worst days, but one of my best days since she became pregnant. I finally was able to release the heavy burden off my back. It was tough, but God carried me through. That same year, the company that I worked for was once again sold to the corporation that I worked for till my separation. Further in the book, I will talk about my separation from the business where I began on October 20, 1980 and worked till April 07, 2006. If anyone would ask me if would ever be out of work I would definitely tell them, "Not in a million years." Guess what! I will be out of job for a year. I would be sitting where a number of people sat, in the unemployment category, and I would be standing in the unemployment lines for long hours. I firmly believe that losing my job was to fulfill the purpose of the book. According to the Bible: "And we know that in all things God works for the good of those who love him, who have been called according to his purpose" (Romans 8:28 NIV). In French: *Nous savons, du reste, que toutes choses concourent au bien de ceux qui aiment Dieu, de ceux qui sont appelés selon son dessein (Louis Segond Translation).*

PICTURE SECTION

age 16

*dad, young
Rev. Pastor Joel J. Esperance*

in Miragoane

dad, older sister Giscelaine, and mom

our house in Miragoane built in 1963

dad, mom, Paul, Bob, Ruth

old church rebuilt in early 70's

new church as of 2004

*with my sisters Marie France
and Marie Nicole*

Joel Esperance

with old friends Port-au-Prince

at my peek time in Haiti

with my sister France

first car, Honda '74
in Haiti with girlfriend Kettline

our family wedding photograph

Pere Noel, Keke, Me and the boys in our first house in Ohio, 1989

live on TV5, Ohio

A. A. S. Graduation

attending Metallurgical training seminar

newly married in New York

St. Augustine, FL, Joey, me, Ricky, Ermelyne, Max

le Doyen de la communote Haitienne de l'Ohio, Dr. Max Pierre Gaujean

Keke and me at 50th Birthday Party

dad, age 90

mom, age 77

my brother, best friend Renel, and dad